The Prince and The Pauper

The Prince and The Pauper

The Case Against Clarence Thomas, Associate Justice of The U.S. Supreme Court

John L. Cooper, Ph.D., John Jay College of Criminal Justice, The City University of New York

Writer's Showcase

San Jose New York Lincoln Shanghai

The Prince and The Pauper
The Case Against Clarence Thomas, Associate Justice of
The U.S. Supreme Court

Writer's Showcase
an imprint of iUniverse.com, Inc.

For information address:
iUniverse.com, Inc.
5220 S 16th, Ste. 200
Lincoln, NE 68512
www.iuniverse.com

ISBN: 0-595-17179-6

Printed in the United States of America

FOREWORD

The name of Clarence Thomas, Associate Justice of the Supreme Court, was frequently mentioned during the Presidential race in 2000. The Republican candidate, George W. Bush, spoke of Justice Thomas with great admiration. Mr. Bush implied that if he became President, he would likely appoint Justices to the High Court who were of the same judicial and political philosophy as Thomas. For this reason, Justice Thomas became an issue in the presidential race. The Democrats, behind their candidate Al Gore, saw Justice Thomas as a right wing ideologue because he had been a lightning rod for criticism since he entered federal government service during the first administration of Ronald Reagan. But the nature of his contentious background was not fully known to the public at large. Because Justice Thomas is a relatively young man, and he will be an influence on the Court for decades to come, the American people should have a better understanding of his history as a public servant.

The following essay, *The Prince and The Pauper*, was written in the Fall of 1991. The purpose of the essay was to try and explain the undercover, political process that brought Clarence Thomas to the door of the Supreme Court. It was written during the Senate confirmation hearings for the nominee, and it was my intention to try and capture the political atmosphere of the time. In particular, I wanted to expose the crosscurrents of debate, from the left and the right that influenced that atmosphere. I proceeded in this manner because the political context is important in understanding Clarence Thomas' behavior then and I believe even now. I make this assertion because Justice Thomas is truly a creature of the political process in Washington, D.C.

PREFACE

This essay, *The Prince and The Pauper*, was written specifically as a bill of indictment against Clarence Thomas and the self-serving political process in our nation's capital. It was this same process that nurtured the conservative philosophy of Thomas; and eventually, it helped to elevate him to the Highest Court in the land. However, Judge Thomas was not qualified to be an Associate Justice of the Supreme Court. Indeed, in a published report in the *Legal Times* (8/26/91), a Distinguished Professor of Legal Ethics at Hofstra University Law School said that Thomas was "unfit to sit" on the Supreme Court because in 1990 "he wrote an opinion for the U.S. Court of Appeals for the D.C. Circuit in violation of a federal statute that required him to disqualify himself on ethical grounds."

As an Appellate Court Judge, Thomas' unethical behavior was but one example in a public career that exhibited an extraordinary high degree of malfeasance. Consequently, it is the specific purpose of this essay to offer evidence to substantiate a call for the impeachment of Justice Thomas. Believe me, I say this in all seriousness, and I will support the call with a variety of independent reports. But first, before I began to present my information, let me clarify my initial narrative technique.

As I begin this indictment, some very strong statements and conclusions will be made about the behavior of Clarence Thomas. Some readers may find these preliminary interjections disconcerting. The comments would seem to be unjustified because no basis for them has yet been established. But, these statements and conclusions will give us insight into the possible reasons for Clarence Thomas' behavior as a conservative ideologue, a public servant, and a black man. The reader needs to be aware of these allegations, and the statements about his personality at the outset, because I use them to develop my arguments throughout this paper.

Lastly, the Prince in the title of this essay refers to Presidents Ronald Reagan and George H. Bush. It relies upon the concept of the *imperial presidency*. The Prince, as an idea, is not a definite depiction of a person in the White House. It speaks more to the personification of the arrogance of power, and the name and description of the Prince is taken from the work of Niccolo Machiavelli. Clarence Thomas is metaphorically presented as the Pauper.

From Machiavelli's book, the Prince was a political manipulator who used people and the governmental system to serve his personal, devious ends. Mr. Reagan and Mr. Bush used Clarence Thomas in this fashion. The two Presidents played upon his desire to relieve himself of his ethnic and social pauperism.

INTRODUCTION

In his book *The Prince*, Niccolo Machiavelli spoke of amoral political behavior in government as a means of redemption for a weak, anomic society that had broken loose from its Christian moorings. Such behavior, he believed, was consistent with basic human nature. Humans are ungrateful, fickle, lying, hypocritical, fearful and grasping creatures. Consequently, social order does not develop from the good will of the people; but rather, institutions of legitimate authority are forced upon them.

Machiavellian political principles and methods are characterized by expediency, craftiness and duplicity. Circumstances are governed by the moment, and the end justifies the means. Therefore, in government, the ship of state is merely a tool to be used by its leader, the Prince. At the same time, Machiavelli was nobody's fool. He understood the ambiguity of this elitist outlook, but he was also a realist, a pragmatist, and a cynic. Overall, it was his cynicism that shaped his view of human behavior in government, and that behavior is always cloaked in a convenient rationale. Above all else, the Republic must be protected and saved.

Machiavelli has been in his grave for over 400 years, but his political principles live on. Americans were witness to them anew with the nomination of Judge Clarence Thomas, a black man, to be an Associate Justice of the Supreme Court, by President George H. Bush. What a shock! By any legal standard, or by any stretch of the legal imagination, Judge Thomas did not appear to be qualified.

Moreover, as a member of the executive branch of government in the Reagan and Bush administrations, Clarence Thomas was guilty of flagrant abuses of governmental authority that were probably unparalleled in the history of bureaucratic administration in Washington. His record was replete with examples of nonfeasance, misfeasance, and malfeasance in the exercise of his official, public duties. At one point, his behavior was so recalcitrant; he refused to carry out a court order while Assistant Secretary for Civil Rights at the Department of Education.

As a public servant, an administrator of two important government agencies in the field of civil rights enforcement, at the Department of Education and the Equal Employment Opportunity Commission (EEOC), Thomas conducted himself as a biased, self-serving, opinionated petulant ideologue. In a bizarre sense of dedication to principles, he often campaigned and spoke out against the very same policies he had been sworn to implement.

In his capacity as a top administrator, he enjoyed wielding power, but even more importantly he relished having individuals show respect for his power. He had a tremendous need for self-aggrandizement, and if the use of his power hurt others, so be it. In this regard, he was consistently self-righteous, arrogant and petty towards the people he had been empowered to serve. By any account, he was an uncaring, unsympathetic public administrator. Accordingly, as the chief enforcement officer for affirmative action at the EEOC, he was an unmitigated disaster and a civil rights nightmare.

Nevertheless, in spite of his insensitive, socially obnoxious administrative record, Thomas was appointed to the Court of Appeals in February, 1990. He would have only a short tenure at the Court of Appeals because, astonishingly, he was nominated for the Supreme Court in July 1991. Therefore, contrary to the statement by President Bush, that his nominee was the best-qualified jurist he could find to sit on the Supreme Court, Thomas was seriously lacking in judicial experience. Furthermore, as his government service indicated, it would seem that he was temperamentally unsuited to be on the High Court.

And, make no mistake about it; having an unqualified person on the Supreme Court will be demeaning to that Court. The presence of

Thomas on the High Bench will undoubtedly lower the standards of that judicial assembly and bring disrepute to that august institution. As a consequence, with the passage of time, the public may come to lose respect for the institution.

However, there is a much greater problem confronting the American people now that Thomas is a member of the Supreme Court. His public behavior would suggest that he is a person who has an excitable, petty psychological profile. An aberrant manner can be noted in his attitude and conduct when he worked for the Reagan and Bush administrations. Throughout his tenure at the Department of Education and the EEOC, he was embroiled in controversy concerning the interpretation and implementation of civil rights law and the enforcement of affirmative action guidelines. Ignoring his legal responsibilities, he frequently disobeyed the mandates of Congress and the courts. In a haughty fashion, he would let it be known to all concerned that he, Clarence Thomas, knew what was best for the public being served.

As well, he would often provoke controversy by refusing to carry out his sworn duties. When challenged, he would then blame the dispute on the liberals, the civil rights organizations and the black leadership. Those other groups inspired the controversy because they did not like him. As a conservative republican in the executive branch of government, he saw himself as personally serving President Ronald Reagan, and apparently he felt that Mr. Reagan's ideological enemies were his enemies, too.

Consistent with his psychological profile, Thomas had a very strong tendency for self-reference. As an administrator, when problems and situations would develop, to the exclusion of others, like his support staff at two government agencies, he would rely almost entirely upon himself to engender the proper response, and more often then not, his personal solution would be characterized as the best solution. Moreover, being a supervisor of a government agency, he tended to be rigid and dictatorial with his subordinates. Everything had to be just right with them. He was a no nonsense leader with his troops, but as an administrator who was a public servant, he was impudent and negligent to the people he was suppose to serve.

In personality terms, Thomas presented himself as a strong, self-possessed leader-bureaucrat who was a perfectionist and a person who had an exaggerated sense of self-importance. These attitudes were also coupled with feelings that his own people did not respect him. The pattern suggests that he suffers from a disturbed, psychological profile. Individuals with such a profile possess the potential to exhibit irrational, and even bizarre, behavior when under stress.

As the final arbiters of the American constitutional system, the Justices of the Supreme Court collectively exercise a tremendous influence on the destiny of America unequaled by any other branch of government.[i] In the coming years, the Court will be rendering decisions on abortion, civil rights, writs of habeas corpus, the electoral process, term limitations for elected officials, and much, much more. These decisions will help to determine the future of America. As a result, the Court will be under severe scrutiny, and the Justices will be experiencing a great deal of public pressure to make decisions that serve the common good.

Clarence Thomas will be one of those Justices, and given his psychological profile, there is no way to estimate how he will react to the new mantle of power bestowed upon him and the accompanying pressure that would also be draped over his shoulders. Yes, he is only one Justice in nine, but Thomas has demonstrated that he has a strong, dominating, perhaps even charismatic, personality. Friends, associates and individuals who worked with him, have tended to develop an unyielding admiration for the man.

What influence might he have with his fellow justices of the Supreme Court? Who can really say? But if his performance before the Judiciary Committee of the U.S. Senate is any indication, it may be persuasive. He seems to have the ability to mesmerize people, especially individuals who believe in him and the conservative, political cause he articulates. Members of the Judiciary Committee certainly followed his lead during his testimony before that body. But, of course, the Committee members were influenced by certain political concerns.

The question is, should the American people have confidence in a Supreme Court that may be unduly influenced by a possibly paranoid, charismatic individual. Moreover, is this the kind of man that should sit on the Highest Court in the land? President Bush thought so, and that is why he nominated him for the job. But, make no mistake about it, Thomas was nominated solely for expedient, partisan political reasons. Bush had his own *Princely*, hidden agenda, and Thomas was to be his *agent*.

Nevertheless, President Bush should have understood that Machiavelli's governmental principles were not designed to be used in democratic, political precincts. People power can thwart the will of the Prince. This is why, during the nominating process of Clarence Thomas, our government functioned from behind a veil of hypocrisy and subterfuge.

Nevertheless, there has always been some Machiavelli's principles mixed into our governmental system. Beginning with the writing of the U.S. Constitution, the American people have never quite received what they were promised. For instance, they are not really allowed to hold the electoral reins of power. The Electoral College was instituted to keep essential power in the hands of the chosen few.

However, the Machiavellians of our day should be reminded of the cost of forsaking democratic institutions. Apparently, they are unaware of the fact that there is a functional relationship between a moral society and a democratic government. In the context of the American Republic, there can not be one without the other. Moreover, for a representative democracy like that of the United States, officials in government must carry out their duties and responsibilities in an ethical and moral manner; or there can be no government of the people, by the people, and for the people as Lincoln spoke of it.

Moral behavior requires a person to do the right thing in respect to others. Essentially for our government officials, this means serving the constituent population as defined by statute, law, and oath of office.

Without moral guidance, our government will serve itself; and the people in it, the public servants, are likely to become blinded by political and careerist tunnel-vision. And then, they will use the government for self-interested purposes.

There are those who say that our centralized, federal system of government invites antidemocratic abuses. To be sure, there was much opposition to the creation of a national government at the time the U.S. Constitution was being ratified. Voices of the people could be heard saying the Framers of the Constitution had gone too far. By their design, the natural course of power was to make the many slaves of the few, and the bulk of the people would have little to say about it. Consequently, the new government would not be a government of the people. In the end, the elites will struggle for power, honor and wealth; and the poor will become nothing more then prey to avarice, insolence and oppression.

The people who opposed ratification of the U.S. Constitution were known as the anti-federalists. They saw a national government as becoming a political bastion for the rich elites. In particular, they thought that the Presidency had been given too much power. The President would be an elected king, "vested with power dangerous to a free people," and as well they thought the Electoral College was "an aristocratic junta." There were also complaints that the structure of the federal government seem to "verge too much toward the British plan;" that the relation between the Senate and President looked too much like a king and a House of Lords, and it all equaled an oligarchy.[ii]

The fears of the anti-federalist would seem to have been borne out with the nomination and confirmation to the Supreme Court of the former bureaucrat Clarence Thomas.

The anti-federalists also recognized that a very fragile process constitutes a political democracy. It is open to abuse as a consequence of its egalitarian philosophy. There are always strained relations in government because of the conflicts between the rights of the individual versus the rights of the group and the idea of the common good. Moreover, if there is to be government, there must also be respect for authority by the citizenry. Working for the common good usually means maintaining traditions, generally keeping things as they are, or more specifically maintaining the status quo. Therefore, government by its nature is more conservative then liberal.

As well, America is a multi-ethnic society of haves and have-nots, of mainstream and peripheral communities. Nevertheless, democratic government is expected to treat everyone the same, but is this realistic? And is it possible, given the conservative tendencies of government?

History tells us that our government tends to serve a conservative ideology best, and you can be sure that Machiavelli would have classified himself as a political conservative. The reason, on both accounts, is obvious. Liberalism is anathema to the maintenance of the status quo and the redemption of the Republic, as Machiavelli would have it.

Beginning with Ronald Reagan, for over a decade, the people of the United States listened to conservative politicians calling for social policies that would save the American Republic. There should be more guns and less butter. The social programs of government should bend to the theory of supply-side economics, and affirmative action programs for minorities should be eliminated. No more quotas.

Yes, the Prince from Hollywood made governmental change seem so necessary. He preached with such self-righteousness because history seemed to be on his side, and Clarence Thomas was there to help him save America.

To the conservative call, the American people responded by electing Ronald Reagan and George Bush to the White House, and these two Presidents have sailed their ships of state with a steady breeze of amorality and professional impropriety; e.g., the secret contra-war in Nicaragua, the bombing of Tripoli and Benghazi in Libya, the Iran-contra affair, and the scandal in the Department of Housing and Urban Development under Secretary Samuel R. Pierce, Jr. For the greater good, Reagan and Bush offered the country feudalistic leadership based on a philosophy of *noblesse oblige*.

Clarence Thomas was a political product of the Reagan and Bush years in Washington, and he was an operative for the ultra-conservative leadership of the Republican Party. His elevation to the Supreme Court came about not because he was "the best man for the job," but rather because he was a part of a larger strategy to reclaim the Republic and save it from degrading, unchristian liberalism.

Given Thomas' track record as a maleficent bureaucrat and a conservative ideologue, there was strong opposition to his nomination to the Supreme Court. The opposition came from Congress, civil rights organizations and generally liberal organizations across the land. There was recognition by pundits, high and low, that the Prince was packing the Court with yet another political partisan. President Bush just smiled and said that Judge Thomas was the best man for the job.

But, should the Supreme Court be for or against any political philosophy? Should the Court not have a neutral bias? Rather then taking sides, the Court must stand for the ultimate morality in the administration of justice. It must be perceived as being fair and impartial in its decision-making. The legal structure of the nation, and the confidence of the people in the institution depend upon it.

Newsweek Magazine stated the case this way: "The Supreme Court commands neither purse nor sword. It is the bystander branch of the federal government, deriving authority simply from the mystic trust of the people that it rules by reason and a law higher than political calculation. How else can the court work its will on such issues as flag-burning and school prayer, where the political branches so clearly believe judge-made constitutional low is flat wrong?"[iii]

Now that Thomas sits on the High Bench, the moral efficacy of the Court will definitely be in question. Not only was he an expedient, political choice for the Court, but during the confirmation hearings he was accused of sexual harassment by a former, female subordinate. The harassment allegedly occurred when he worked with the woman at the

Department of Education and the EEOC. Thomas denied the allegations. But, they were not satisfactorily refuted and they probably never will be.

The allegations went with him to the Supreme Court, and now a moral cloud of suspicion hangs over his head. Whether or not it is because of his maleficent behavior as a public servant or an unethical, indifferent nature to truth and respect for others, Clarence Thomas will never be able to exculpate himself from the image that he possibly committed grievous social, if not legal, sins. As long as he sits on the Supreme Court, the moral stature of that institution will suffer.

In this context, Newsweek had this to say, "For the worst reasons, Thomas is now the best-known member of the Court. If, through wisdom of his judging, Thomas rises above the moral cloud, the din of recent events will fade from memory. If not, the Supreme Court stands to lose the public faith that ultimately grants it legitimacy.[iv]

The day before the Senate voted to confirm Clarence Thomas as an Associate Justice of the Supreme Court, a number of national polls reported that a majority of the American people supported him for the seat on the Court. The American people were quite wrong in their assessment of Clarence Thomas, but they are to be forgiven because they did not have all the facts concerning the sordid background of this man. If they had known the truth about him, I am confident the American people would not have supported his elevation to the High Court. I also firmly believe that if the true character of the man had been exposed, black Americans would have rejected him out of hand also.

At the same time, President Bush must have known about the unethical, sordid background of judge Thomas. There was the FBI reports to read and discussions with members of Congress who had the opportunity to interact with him and observe his record through the exercise of their oversight of those agencies within the Executive Branch to which he had been appointed.[v] As well, Bush and Thomas had been members of Executive Branch of government for nine years in the Reagan and Bush administrations. They knew of each other because both of them were committed to the same social philosophy. Consequently, it must be concluded that Bush did not care about his shoddy, inexperienced malfeasance record. Thomas was on the side of the Prince and that was enough.

And what of Clarence Thomas himself? He knew about his own background because he lived it, and being a lawyer, having attended one of the finest law schools in the country, he knew that he was unqualified to serve on the Supreme Court. And, if Thomas were a man of honor and integrity, he would have refused the nomination when President Bush first offered it to him, but he wanted to be on the Supreme Court. And, he probably thought of the nomination as a reward for services rendered to two Presidents.

In any event, that is in the past. Today, now, what should Associate Justice of the Supreme Court, Clarence Thomas do to begin to recover his lost dignity and honor? He should resign from the Supreme Court forthwith. However, I know that Justice Thomas will not resign from the Court. Therefore, it is left to me to make the case as to why he should be removed from the Court in the legal manner prescribed by the Constitution of the United States. Justice Thomas should be impeached.

Government exhibited a very ugly, undemocratic face during the Clarence Thomas Supreme Court nomination hearing. This is due to the fact that maleficent behavior has been on the increase in government for decades. The recognition of this fact inspired me to ask a question: Is democracy, as the founding fathers envisioned it, viable in America today? Based on the Clarence Thomas debacle, the answer would seem to be no. The most important reasons for this conclusion are: 1) The capitalistic, multicultural nature of the American polity; 2) racial politics, and 3) the strong influence of partisan politics in government affairs. All three of these forces contributed significantly to the Thomas fiasco.

Before I present the details of the facts in this case against Justice Thomas, let me make a few preparatory, thesis remarks. The reader is reminded that the anti-federalists warned the American people about a government that could produce an "aristocratic tyranny," in which the elites of society would struggle with the non-elites. This is essentially what happened in the Thomas nomination hearings. Specifically, the non-elites were destined to lose the struggle because the elites had hidden agendas.

BACKGROUND

Clarence Thomas was born in Pin Point, Georgia in 1948. He was the grandson of a sharecropper. Growing up in the rural South, early in his life, he learned to live with poverty and racism. As well, Southern society was dominated by a rigid caste system, in which white supremacy ruled, and whites had little respect for black people. Blacks were expected to stay in their place, and if they did that, they would be tolerated.

From the age of seven, his grandfather, who sent him to Catholic schools, raised Thomas. He was told that hard work and self-reliance could overcome any obstacle discrimination might put in his way, if he was willing to pay the price.[vi] His grandfather had a very strong influence on his life, and he taught him many values that helped to shape the personality of the man Clarence Thomas has become.

Being a youth in the 1950s and '60s, Thomas was witness, up close, to the struggle for freedom in the civil rights movement. Dixie was undergoing change. The South was in social turmoil. The Jim Crow structure of the system was under attack. Many white Southerners were frightened, and they were experiencing a great deal of anxiety about their future; and many people, both black and white, were suffering from a deep sense of anomie.

It is very likely that Clarence Thomas also suffered from a feeling of anomie. His hard work and self-reliance was not likely to be appreciated in a time of extreme racial tensions and social instability. And, strange as it may seem, his perception could have led him to believe that the civil rights movement was responsible. Everyone was being asked to take sides. The liberals were expected to favor an expansion of civil rights for black

Americans. The conservatives were required to support the status quo or a more moderate rate of desired social change for Negroes. The path of liberalism was strewn with instability and uncertainty. The path of conservatism would ostensibly relieve society of the racial tensions, social instability, and return the system to the social equilibrium of the past.

In the heat of the civil rights debate, it is easy to understand why Clarence Thomas was confused about the ideology he should follow, but because of the values he learned from his grandfather, his inclination was probably to follow the conservative line. In any event, as is the case with many young people, he oscillated between various political viewpoints until he found the niche that would serve his needs.

From a Catholic education, Thomas learned endearing respect for church authority and a higher law than men. The Catholic Church taught its followers to believe in its doctrinal completeness, its ability to adapt to the needs of humankind, and its moral and spiritual perfection. The Church was a stabilizing force in his life, and it tended to re-enforce his conservative inclinations,

Thomas attended Holy Cross College, and he spent eight months studying for the priesthood at Immaculate Conception Seminary in Missouri before going on to Yale Law School. He left the Seminary because of a negative comment made by a fellow student on the assassination of Martin Luther King, Jr.

Throughout his youthful years in the 1960s, Thomas did not identify with the political causes of black people. Indeed, he put distant between himself and the black community. He did not involve himself in the civil rights movement to any appreciable extent, and in an interview he acknowledged going through a period of "self-hate," during which he tried to fit in (to white society) by avoiding every form of stereotypical black behavior.[vii]

Thomas' background would suggest that he has been running from his blackness, and he has been in search of respect and stability. But, he may also be suffering from Shelby Steele's notion of "integration shock;" that is, "the intense feelings of racial inferiority and self-doubt that can assault and sometimes overwhelm blacks who, like Thomas, were suddenly taken from their familiar surroundings and plunged into a previously all-white and not always welcoming world."[viii]

Blacks who confront this phenomenon may experience a number of psychological disorientations, psychiatrists say. They may angrily repudiate whites or they may develop an emotional identification with whites so complete they exhibit a "bleaching syndrome," in which they deny any connection with blacks. There is also the Token Black Syndrome, a reaction to white backlash against affirmative action. With this disorder, successful black persons delude themselves into believing they have made it solely because they are exceptionally gifted individuals who are innately superior to less fortunate members of their race. These persons will often chastise poor blacks, especially those who are on welfare or who have given birth to a child out of wedlock. If these poor blacks were more like them, intelligent instead of stupid, hard working instead of lazy, educated instead of ignorant, morally upright instead of being slovenly, racial progress would have been assured a long time ago.

Growing up in a de jure segregated South, Clarence Thomas sought recognition and respect from whites. They held power in society, and in his eyes only they could truly acknowledge his worth. However, for a black man to be successful he must demonstrate to whites that he is not a threat to them. This approach exposes the black person's spin on the survival of the fittest idea. In a word, its known as *OpporTOMism*.[ix]

As Assistant Secretary for Civil Rights at the Department of Education

Clarence Thomas graduated from Yale Law School in 1974. As a student there, he kept away from classes that dealt with racial issues. He concentrated on classes that were concerned with corporate issues. He specifically distanced himself from classes on civil rights, and upon graduating; he turned down bids from firms that offered to let him do pro bono work for good causes. Instead, he settled on a position in the Missouri state attorney general's office, where he handled revenue and tax cases.[x] The attorney general, at the time, was John Danforth.

Thomas changed jobs in 1977 when he went to work for Monsanto, the huge chemical company. He worked for Monsanto for only a short while. In 1979, he moved to Washington, D.C. to become a legislative aide on energy and environmental matters for the now U.S. Senator John Danforth. In 1980, he functioned as a member of President-elect Reagan's transition team. Along with others, he had the responsibility of evaluating EEOC policies that supported equal employment opportunities and policies that protected workers from sexual harassment.

In May 1981, President Reagan appointed Thomas to be Assistant Secretary for Civil Rights at the Department of Education. With this appointment, civil rights enforcement under the Reagan administration became nothing more than cold acts of white-collar intimidation and failure. Bureaucratic arrogance and administrative maliciousness reached heights of intolerance never before seen in official Washington, and it

4

was to last for almost nine years under the pernicious tutelage of Clarence Thomas.

> The civil rights office of the Education Department is responsible for enforcing Title VI of the Civil Rights Act of 1964 and Title IX of the Education Amendments of 1973. It is responsible for insuring that institutions that discriminate on the basis of race, sex, handicap and age do not receive student aid, Chapter I grants and other federal funds. It uses federal financial assistance as a carrot and a stick to insure equal opportunity for a quality education in the 16,000 school systems, 3,200 colleges and universities, 10,000 proprietary institutions (for-profit schools for career preparation) and other types of institutions such as libraries and museums that receive Education Department funds.[xi]

Thomas' tenure at the Office of Civil Rights (OCR) began on a negative note. OCR had been under court order since 1970 to implement desegregation remedies and to assist black colleges in making up for their neglect by southern state governments in the past.[xii] The court order ensued from the case of Adams v. Bell, and it was clear in its statement that institutions, which received federal funds, must do more then just adopt nondiscriminatory policies. They must take affirmative action steps.

Within the first few months at OCR, Thomas began undermining the enforcement of the Adam's court order. He began to negotiate individually with states and this gave them a free hand in dealing with desegregation. In taking this negotiating track, OCR abandoned established guidelines that in fact had the force of law; and as a result, Thomas allowed each state to determine if desegregation had occurred.

In response to the failure of OCR to enforce the Adam's court order, women and minority plaintiffs, in the spring of 1982, brought contempt charges against the Department of Education. In particular, the Department was accused of refusing to investigate discrimination complaints and perform compliance reviews in a timely manner. The counter argument made by the Department was that they did not need court supervision.

Testifying for the Department, Clarence Thomas told the court that he did not think investigating discrimination complaints could be done in a timely manner. He said he was studying the matter, but he did not know when his study would be complete. Additionally, in response to Judge John H. Pratt's questions, Thomas gave the following answers.

> Q: ...But you're going ahead and violating those time frames; is that true? You're violating them in compliance reviews on all occasions, practically, and you're violating them on complaints most of the time, or half the time; Isn't that true?
>
> A: That's right.
>
> Q: So aren't you, in effect, substituting your judgment as to what the policy should be for what the court order requires? The court order requires you to comply with this 90 day period; isn't that true?
>
> A: That's right.
>
> Q: And you have not imposed a deadline (for an Office of Civil Rights study of lack of compliance with the Adams order); is that correct?
>
> A: I have not imposed a deadline.
>
> Q: And meanwhile, you are violating a court order rather grievously, aren't you?
>
> A: Yes.[xiii]

Of course, Thomas could refuse to comply with the Adams order because he was acting under the protection of his Prince. The federal government was being impacted by the *Reagan revolution*. There was this attitude among members of the Executive Branch that one had to serve the President first and the people second, and this was no mean exaggeration. The Reagan administration did appoint people, like Clarence Thomas, to disfavored offices with the task of sabotaging the work of those offices.[xiv]

However, the recalcitrant acts of Thomas were so legally disturbing, even the Reagan Department of Justice protested the failure of OCR to enforce civil rights laws. Thomas received a letter from the Assistant Attorney General William Bradford Reynolds in which he objected to the use of "hold" categories to immobilize the processing of complaints and requesting that he notify OCR employees to "begin accepting, investigating and, where appropriate, remedying" them.[xv] Nevertheless, even though he had been instructed by the Justice Department to, in effect, comply with the Adams court order, Thomas refused to carry out his duties under the law.

Knowing that the conservative, Republican administration of Ronald Reagan did not want expeditious enforcement of civil rights laws, OCR under Clarence Thomas developed a procedure known as "Early Complaint Resolution." This procedure was supposedly designed to settle civil rights complaints before there was an investigation. The Justice Department wrote to Thomas to say that Early Complaint Resolution might not meet applicable standards and "could lead to a weakening of your enforcement posture and our litigating position," but Thomas made no changes in the procedure.[xvi]

Early Complaint Resolution came under scrutiny in 1985 by a House Committee. It was reported that 312 cases had been settled using the procedure, and OCR could not show that "any or all of the settlements were in accordance with statutory or regulatory requirements." The House Committee stated that the use of Early Complaint Resolution "may be illegal, may not protect the rights of complainants, and may jeopardize future litigation involving violations of civil rights laws."[xvii]

It is difficult to believe that Thomas' administrative failure at OCR was an accident. It seems that he was placed in OCR to decapitate civil rights enforcement at the Department of Education. This would make him a saboteur, and he carried out his assignment with eagerness. His arrogance could only have meant that he thoroughly enjoyed exercising the power of his office against the people he was supposed to serve. With just one procedure, he could affect the lives of many people and make them bow to his will.

Thomas had extremely negative proclivities in expressing his administrative power, and he seemed to have a particularly strong animus towards civil rights laws and their enforcement. He even flaunted his administrative inclinations in the face of the Supreme Court.

In 1975, the federal government issued regulations that prohibited universities and other grantees of federal funds from discriminating in employment on the basis of gender.[xviii] In 1981, a challenge to the regulations came before the Supreme Court, and while the Justice Department was defending the Department of Education's rules on the subject in the Supreme Court, the head of OCR, Clarence Thomas, announced that the Education Department was going to reverse its policy and declare that the anti-gender discrimination law did not apply to employment.[xix] Fortunately for the American people, the Justice Department rejected this proposal, and the Supreme Court upheld the regulation, finding that the anti-gender-bias laws did apply to employment.[xx]

Thomas was at the Department of Education for barely a year, but in that short space of time, he altered, for the worse, its major civil rights enforcement policies. For instance, he failed to implement provisions that would have funneled millions of dollars into the historically Black colleges. Because of his anti-civil rights posture at OCR, Black colleges and universities saw their funds from the state governments drastically cut and steps taken to make them noncompetitive in every state in the South.

For his own self-aggrandizement and the need to ingratiate himself with his Prince, Thomas allowed himself to be used as a negative force against black schools in the South and desegregation in higher education. The steps he took at OCR led to increasing budget reductions, admission constraints and other impediments that strangle Black public colleges and universities today. In good Machiavellian moves, duplicitous actions by Thomas led to the 1988 announcement by William Bennett (then-Secretary of the Department of Education) that the southern states were all in compliance and had desegregated higher education completely.[xxi] What a lie!

As Chairman of the Equal Employment Opportunity Commission

In the ideological testing ground of the Department of Education, Clarence Thomas had proved to the powers that be that he was willing to disregard his own people in order to support the Reagan revolution. The Reagan Administration was in the process of saving American society from New Deal Liberalism that had captured the heart of government almost fifty years ago, and it did not matter that New Deal Liberalism had saved America from the conservative, Republican policies that gave us the Great Depression. That was then. Today, the government and the nation had drifted too far to the left, towards Godless socialism.

From the conservative point of view, the people had to be weaned from debilitating, liberal policies. Therefore, during the Reagan Presidency, administrative negativism was taken as being a positive when it was directed at liberals, racial minorities, and the collective have-nots in general. Because he had done so well in this fashion at OCR, the Reagan Administration wanted to give Clarence Thomas a larger role in the subversion efforts to undermine civil rights laws and their implementation policies.

Early on in 1982, Thomas was nominated to head the EEOC. He was confirmed as its Chairman in May of that year. The EEOC is the agency with the major responsibility for enforcing federal laws that guarantee equal employment opportunity. Specifically, it seeks remedies for age, sex, handicap, religion, national origin and race discrimination. Clarence Thomas had now become the chief enforcement officer for civil rights in the nation. He was to hold this office for two four-year terms, and he was a master at creating controversy during his tenure.

At OCR, Thomas had deliberately disobeyed a court order from the Adams case, substituting his judgment for the courts, even though as he admitted in federal court, the beneficiaries under the civil rights laws would have been helped by compliance with the court order.[xxii] This type of self-reference he brought with him to the EEOC, and it would play an important role in his decision-making at that agency.

However, as Chairman of the EEOC, Thomas had been recruited to play a more direct role in the Reagan revolution, and as a consequence of his policies at the EEOC, private industry began to regain its hiring controls over the work force. This control had been substantially affected by civil rights laws, which required the increased inclusion of racial minorities and women in the work place.

The Reagan revolution was based on the conservative philosophy of supply-side economics. There was to be a return to the free market, laissez-faire economy of the pre-New Deal days. It was the family-bound, white males who had been pillars of strength in the traditional free market economy. If America was going to be saved from over-worked liberalism, there had to be a return to this occupational tradition.

Thomas' work at the EEOC is usually evaluated on the basis of his personal opposition to affirmative action, in particular to the uses of "goals and timetables" associated with numerical remedies to past patterns of discrimination.[xxiii] It is believed that his opposition evolved from the radical individualism that he embraces which is of a type that has been related to the 19th century laissez-faire capitalists; his belief in self-help as it illuminates himself as a self-made man; and his belief in a higher or natural law which seems to be a twist on the fundamental idea of social Darwinism.

At the same time, when evaluating his record at the EEOC, it should be kept in mind that he was out to trash the rationale for affirmative action and to stop the implementation of such policies in an effort to help white males maintain their primacy in the occupational system. Indeed,

Thomas' decision-making and behavior at the EEOC begin to make sense only when viewed from within this context.

When he became head of the EEOC, Thomas made it known that he would devise a new policy-formation for dealing with job discrimination. This new policy-formation would focus on the individual and acts of discrimination against individuals. He said that the emphasis of the Commission would be on making individual victims of discrimination whole. He reasoned in the following manner: "In the past, the Commission has chosen to concentrate on prospective relief in the form of numerical goals and timetables, rather than full relief for the party actually filing the charge. I find it ironic that anyone would put a policy in place which provided less for those who were *actually* hurt then for those who *may* have been hurt as a result of historical events."[xxiv]

With his focus on the individual, Chairman Thomas had devised a perfect strategy to challenge the basic legal program used by the agency to confront discrimination in employment. Once it became operational, the new policy had a chilling effect upon the productive work of the EEOC. For instance, it reduced the amount of systemic or class-action litigation carried on by the agency. Class-action suits were one of the best ways to fight and eliminate institutionalized patterns of job discrimination against minorities and women.[xxv]

The effectiveness of the strategy used by Thomas can be seen in the fact that class-action charges decreased substantially during his tenure, despite threats by the House Education and Labor Committee to cut other parts of the EEOC budget because of its failure to pursue systemic remedies, and despite the proven success of such suits, which could bring about industry wide changes of policy and practices.[xxvi]

However, Thomas' hidden agenda is exposed when his focus on the individual is evaluated in terms of the settlement of an actual, important class-action suit. Such a suit had been filed against AT&T charging that its women employees had suffered under discriminatory rules on pregnancy leave. AT&T settled the suit by agreeing to pay $66,000,000 to

13,000 women. Under the Thomas approach, there would have been 13,000 discrimination cases filed against AT&T., and there was the possibility that each case could have been settled differently. But, with the class action settlement arranged by the EEOC, 13,000 women did receive benefits as individuals.

Nevertheless, even with clear evidence of the usefulness of class action suits. Thomas maintained, "Emphasis on 'systemic' suits led the Commission to overlook many of the individuals who came to our offices to file charges and seek assistance."[xxvii] But, this was all a smoke screen because with his professed interest in the rights of the individual claimant, settlement rates of individual claims sank from 32.1% in Fiscal Year 1980 to 13.9% in Fiscal Year 1989.

Moreover, with this new focus at the EEOC, the percentage of cases in which the claimant received no remedy at all rose from 28.5% in Fiscal Year 1980 to 54.2% in the Fiscal Year 1989.[xxviii] In an investigation to determine what brought about this change, the General Accounting Office reported that this increase was not due to a spate of unsubstantiated complaints but to *inadequate investigation,* brought about in part by the perception of the EEOC staff that the Commission was more interested in reducing the case backlog than in full investigation.[xxix]

Another ignominious, backward step taken by Chairman Thomas was that of finding fault with, and as a consequence for all practical purposes eliminating, the EEOC guidelines developed in the 1960s that prohibited employer practices having a disparate impact on minority workers or applicants that could not be justified as measures of effective job performance. The legal principle behind the guidelines had been upheld by the Supreme Court in a unanimous decision in Griggs v. Duke Power Co.[xxx]

The guidelines had even been adopted by a number of federal government agencies, but none of this made any difference to Chairman Thomas. He said, in 1984, that the guidelines encouraged "too much reliance on statistical disparities as evidence of employment discrimination."[xxxi] He threatened to repeal the guidelines, but he never did. Still, the EEOC staff got the message. The Chairman did not favor cases using statistical disparities, no matter how solidly they were based in the law.

On another front, Thomas withdrew the agency's support for the use of "goals and timetables" for eliminating job bias, which had been a significant form of measurable accountability in the EEOC's conciliation agreements and court-approved settlements. Thomas told the agency's Acting General Counsel to direct his legal staff not to seek enforcement of goals and timetables in existing consent decrees and not to write them into future settlements. He was even bold enough to say in 1986, in an article published in the *Washington Post,* "should a consent decree with goals and timetables come before the Commission, it doesn't have the votes. They simply don't get approved.[xxxii]

In the clearest example of how Clarence Thomas was being used as an intergovernmental subversive, as Chairman of the EEOC he refused to carry out his statutory responsibility to oversee the anti-discrimination efforts of the nation's largest employer, the federal government. As a matter of law, all federal agencies are required to give to the EEOC their plans for hiring and promoting minorities and women. These plans must include a profile of the existing workforce, with special attention being given to the barriers to employment opportunities for minorities and women, and how those barriers will be removed.

As required by law, the EEOC must review these plans to ensure effective programs to overcome job discrimination, but Chairman Thomas refused to exercise his legal authority when early in his tenure the Departments of Justice and Education, along with several other agencies, failed to comply with this requirement. When asked to explain his nonfeasance action, he told Congress that he did not have the power to compel compliance from these governmental bodies. Congress then said that it would give the EEOC the authority it needed to carry out the law, but Chairman Thomas declined the offer. Upon second thought, he said he preferred the flexibility of the existing arrangement. This policy change was officially formalized in 1987 when the Chairman issued a management directive which shifted the main responsibility for implementing affirmative action plans to individual agency heads, leaving the EEOC with just a minimal oversight responsibility.[xxxiii]

By introducing new policies, changing old ones, and failing to do his duty, Chairman Thomas was dismantling and gutting the former program mechanism that had garnered some success in the fight against job discrimination. Because of its oversight responsibilities, Congress, by statutory law, had a duty to stop him, but for whatever political reasons that governed, Congress was vary slow getting off the mark and was much too tolerant of his recalcitrant, administrative behavior.

And, Chairman Thomas was not timid in the face of Congress. To be sure, he was a cold, bold reactionary that Congress did not seem to know how to handle. For example, in congressional hearings, he established a pattern of complaining about his agency not being organized properly or not having the necessary resources to perform the investigation of complaints and the enforcement it was required to do under the law. But, at the same time, he would conjure up changes that would cripple the operations of his agency even more.

In this respect, he abandoned the Rapid Charge processing procedure that had been in use at the agency, giving his reason for doing so a 1981 General Accounting Office (GAO) report that wondered whether it might inhibit efforts to end discrimination by over-emphasizing settlements. This seems like it could have been a legitimate concern. However, he did not put in a new procedure that could provide for more expeditious settlements for the victims of discrimination.[xxxiv]

Indeed, he warped the process even more, and this practically brought the settlement of claims to a standstill. With his focus on the individual act of discrimination, Thomas had a policy of requiring a full investigation for every charge within a two-tiered process of review that called for a "no cause" finding from district directors. All "no cause" findings were forwarded to the EEOC headquarters where another investigation of the charge would occur. Because of this difficult process, very few complaints received adequate attention, and as a result from 1983 through 1987 the backlog of cases doubled from 31,500 to about 62,000.

Finally, because of this tremendous backlog of cases, Congress acknowledged this strange state of affairs at the EEOC. Here was the director of a federal agency doing his level best to see that his office did not carry out its primary, official task. If he disagreed with the EEOC's mandate, then why did he take the position of Chairman? The negativism of his decision-making put him at odds with the Congress and the American people. Who did he think he was working for?

In April of 1987, Chairman August Hawkins (D-CA) of the House Committee on Education and Labor requested that the GAO conduct a comprehensive study of the EEOC's enforcement activities and administrative procedures. Subsequently, eight other members of Congress added their names to the request. The study was particularly interested in what impact, if any, Chairman Thomas' philosophical views (in political terms that means ideology) might have had on compromising the EEOC field staff's enforcement activity.[xxxv]

The GAO released its report in October of 1988, and its major finding stated that large percentages of the charges of discrimination that were closed by the EEOC District Offices with no-cause determinations were not fully investigated. The cause for this was two-fold. One, the Commission's full investigation policy created confusion among the staff as to when an investigation had been completed, and two EEOC headquarters imposed quantitative production goals on its field staff, creating an incentive among its investigators to complete a certain number of cases as quickly as possible.

Chairman Thomas was not the least bit taken by the GAO report. He described it as "a hatchet job," and he elaborated further in an interview with the *Los Angles Times*. "It's a shame Congress can use the GAO as a lap dog to come up with anything it wants."[xxxvi] Clarence Thomas was no shrinking violet, and he continued his initiatives against the agency throughout his tenure at the EEOC.[xxxvii]

Black conservatives and neoconservatives have taken umbrage with the description of Clarence Thomas as an OpporTOMist, but let the following example serve as an illustration of the behavior for which he stands accused.

When Thomas first assumed the head of the EEOC, he tended to follow the legal mandate of the agency for over a year. He even gave a speech in 1983 that supported the general principle of affirmative action. "It is settled," he said, "that, as a matter of law, affirmative action including the use of numerical goals, may be used in appropriate circumstances."[xxxviii] Also, on April 15, 1983, he told the House Subcommittee on Employment Opportunities that affirmative action relief was proper not just for identifiable victims, but also as a group remedy in discrimination cases.

But soon after he had made his public statements of support for affirmative action, he changed his position. The change seemed to have come about in an effort to conform to the view's expressed by William Bradford Reynolds, the Assistant Attorney General for Civil Rights. Reynolds was opposed to affirmative action and numerical remedies. White workers strongly objected to numerical remedies because they said it denied to them their constitutional right of equal protection before the law. It was another plank in the efforts to reverse affirmative action programs that were construed as hurting white male workers.

By 1984, Chairman Thomas had made a 180-degree turn on the issue. He consistently took every opportunity to express his opposition to federal laws and regulations requiring affirmative action remedies. The only times he would back off from his opposition would be when there was substantial congressional pressure on the EEOC to conform to its mandate. At his 1986 confirmation hearings for a second four- year term as Chairman of the EEOC, he agreed to change his no enforcement policy, but he never did what he promised.

Clarence Thomas was very outspoken, in testimony he gave to Congress, in speeches that he made, and in his writings as to his opposition to affirmative action remedies. Undoubtedly, this trashing of his agency did have an effect upon the organization's ability to carry out its mandate. At the same time, there were many subtleties to Thomas' efforts to sabotage operations at the EEOC.

Quietly, Chairman Thomas withdrew the agency's support for "goals and timetables." He further advised the agency's legal staff that any class action cases, or even charges, had to identify the actual victims of discrimination, which helped to nullify class action suits. This latter change was part of a new policy standard for evaluating charges. There was to be a new higher standard of proof. The old "reasonable cause to believe" test was eliminated, but no new measurement was put in its place. The result was confusion in the evaluating process.

Orders for some changes were issued orally. This is highly unusual in a bureaucratic, government organization. Nevertheless, it gives us some insight into the character of Clarence Thomas. Oral orders direct our attention to Thomas' need for self-reference, his need to wield power, his aggressive posturing and sense of self-importance. Like the military, verbal orders give immediate recognition to the hierarchy of command, of rank and privileges of superior persons and subordinates.

Thomas issued an oral order for the policy change that affected goals and timetables. He issued another such oral order for the EEOC's renunciation of the adverse impact theory traditionally used to prove discrimination, which was articulated by the U.S. Supreme Court in *Griggs V. Duke Power Co.* Government organizations are just not run this way, says Professor Alfred Blumrosen of the Rutgers University School of Law. He described the process as "government by innuendo, where responsible officials skulk in the corridors of power, hoping that staff will intuit their desires."[xxxix]

Near the end of his first four-year term as head of the EEOC, attempts were made to inform the public about Thomas' rather questionable administrative behavior. In response to several news articles about the Commission's policy of focusing on individual, rather than class charges, a letter was sent to Thomas in March, 1985 from 43 members of the Congress stating their grave concern regarding the EEOC's failure to pursue systemic litigation. Could the EEOC be pursuing this policy line in order to avoid class action suits?[xl] Of course, the members of Congress were correct in their assumption about the intent of the policy, but the worse actions, or inactions, by Clarence Thomas at the EEOC, were yet to come.

Under the Age Discrimination in Employment Act of 1967, Congress had given the EEOC the responsibility to protect the employment rights of aging workers. Throughout his tenure as Chairman, this was an area of responsibility of the agency that Thomas seemed most reluctant to become involved with. For example, there were regulations that allowed employers to end their contributions to the pension accounts of employees who had worked on after the age of 65. The regulations would seem to have been in violation of the Age Discrimination in Employment Act, (ADEA) and therefore they probably should have been rescinded by the EEOC. However, there was some legal dispute about the status of the regulations. Finally, in 1986, Congress did pass legislation explicitly prohibiting employers from cutting off pension accruals, credits and contributions for workers over 65, but the delay cost older workers more then $1.5 billion in retirement income over a four-year span.[xli]

In a related matter, Chairman Thomas took the initiative and had the EEOC issue regulations abdicating the agency's responsibility to oversee waivers of employees' rights under the ADEA. Previous to these new regulations on the matter, employers could ask employees to waive their ADEA rights only with the approval of the EEOC. This procedure had been in effect to protect the employees from coercion by employers. These new regulations were in violation of ADEA. Consequently, Congress suspended the regulations for the Fiscal Years 1988,1989, and 1990, but Clarence Thomas as Chairman of the EEOC refused to withdraw or to change the regulation.

The chief responsibility of the EEOC is to protect workers from all types of discrimination, but in the area of age discrimination the record of the EEOC under Thomas was dismal to disastrous. There was an unbelievable neglect of age discrimination charges that had been filed by older workers with the EEOC. Thomas' staff simply failed to complete the processing of many of these complaints within the two-year statute of limitations. As a result, the complaintees lost their right to pursue their claims in court.

And, as if this appalling negligence was not enough, Thomas made matters worse by lying about it, repeatedly, to Congress. When he was asked about how many age discrimination claims had lapsed, he first said only 78. When pressed further, he later said that 900 cases had passed the statute of limitations, and he then continued to revise the figures upward to1, 600, and then to 9,000. Finally, an May1, 1989, before the Senate Committee On Aging, Thomas stated that over 13,000 age discrimination claims had been allowed to expire.[xlii]

Congress was absolutely shocked by this admission of near-criminal negligence on the part of a government official. In an attempt to rescue these older workers' claims, Congress enacted the Age Discrimination Claims Assistance Act in 1988. This law temporarily extended the filing period for age discrimination claims, and it required the EEOC to notify the 13,000 persons affected. The EEOC still did not do its job. "At his confirmation hearing for the Circuit Court of Appeals, Clarence Thomas admitted that thousands of additional claims had lapsed at the EEOC since enactment of the Age Discrimination Claims Assistance Act because they were filed subsequent to the cut-off date of the extension in the Act."[xliii]

To add insult to injury, Chairman Thomas tried to excuse this grievous dereliction of duty by blaming the state and local fair employment agencies with which the EEOC contracted to process many federal employment claims. He argued that the EEOC was not necessarily involved with or responsible for age discrimination claims filed with state or local enforcement agencies.[xliv]

Thomas tried to buttress his argument by further saying "that the lapsing of federal claims was not important because the workers involved still had their state claims that were not subject to the two-year limit. This response was even more troubling than the agency's neglect. The lapse of federal claims is not an unimportant matter. A state law claim is not an adequate substitute for federal rights. Congress enacted the Age Discrimination in Employment Act to give older workers a federal cause of action in federal courts, a cause they could not pursue until processed by the EEOC, and the EEOC had been an obstacle rather than a portal to the realization of those rights. State age discrimination laws often provided less relief then federal law. Furthermore, though the EEOC might contract with state and local agencies to process complaints, that in no way relieved the EEOC of the statutory responsibility to enforce older workers' rights under federal law including monitoring and correcting the activities of its contracted agents. Thomas' attempt to 'pass the buck' to others in this matter does not inspire confidence in his discharge of public responsibilities."xlv

Judging from his actions at the EEOC, Clarence Thomas did not want the public to have confidence in him to discharge his sworn-to responsibilities. It was also apparent that he fostered no confidence in himself to be so responsible. After all, it would seem he was appointed Chairman of the EEOC to fail and not to succeed, and as a subversive he knew what job he was being asked to carry out. He exposed his position time and again in articles he wrote and speeches he made. Almost from the start of his Chairmanship at the EEOC, Thomas carried out a war of words against his own agency and the laws and policies that supported its overall mission.

Thomas was supposed to enforce affirmative action guidelines at the EEOC, but he had this to say about affirmative action. "Why am I opposed to affirmative action? The primary reason I am opposed to it is that I don't see where it solves any problems. As a lawyer, I don't legally see how it is going to be supportable as a social policy for a sufficient period to help black people. We have to sit down and think about the effects of it in the employment arena, when we talk about policies that are race-conscious, particularly the quota system."xlvi

Speaking as Chairman of the EEOC, Thomas made this derogatory comment about his agency. He said it was just as "insane" for blacks to expect relief from the federal government for years of discrimination as it is to expect a mugger to nurse his victim back to health. "Ultimately, the burden of your being mugged falls on you. Now, you don't want it that way, and I don't want it that way. But that's the way it happens…Before affirmative action, how did I make it?"[xlvii]

In respect to the use of goals and timetables as job discrimination remedies, Thomas said, "(American business) has a vested interest in the predictability of goals and timetables…(It) makes your jobs easy and neat, but it's wrong, insulting, and sometimes outright racist."[xlviii] "I continue to believe that distributing opportunities on the basis of race or gender, whoever the beneficiaries, turns the law against employment discrimination on its head. Class preferences are an affront to the rights and dignity of individuals, both those individuals who are directly disadvantaged by them, and those who are their supposed beneficiaries."[xlix]

Thomas has suggested that his objection to affirmative action flows from his understanding of the U.S. Constitution. "I firmly insist," he says, "that the Constitution be interpreted in a colorblind fashion. It is futile to talk of a colorblind society unless this constitutional principle is first established. Hence, I emphasize black self-help, as opposed to racial quotas and other race-conscious legal devices that only further deepen the original problem."[l]

It would seem that Thomas put his legal faith in the Constitution, but that did not apply to the Supreme Court decisions based on its interpretations of the Constitution. His opposition to affirmative action remedies led him to criticize the Supreme Court in three such cases. He said that he had a "personal disagreement with the Court's approval of numerical remedies."[li] Taken together he said the three decisions were an "egregious example" of misinterpretation of the Constitution and legislative intent.[lii] The three cases were Local 28, *Sheet Metal Workers* v. EEOC, 478 U.S.

421 (1986); *Firefighters* v. *Cleveland*, 478 U.S. 501 (1986); and U.S. v. *Paradise*, 480 U.S. 149 (1987).

In another matter, the Johnson Case, which upheld a county plan for increasing the number of women in its workforce, Chairman Thomas expressed the hope that the lower courts would follow the Johnson dissent from the Supreme Court in applying the law.[liii] He also said this about the Johnson decision. "It is just social engineering, and we ought to see it for what it is...We're standing the principle of nondiscrimination on its head, it is as simple as that, and we're standing the legislative history of Title VII on its head."[liv] Title VII of the Civil Rights Act of 1964 specifically authorizes courts to order affirmative action remedies when employers have violated the law.

Also, Chairman Thomas frequently criticized specific Commission proceedings and cases in progress. For example, there was the time when he took the unusual step of criticizing the merits of a then-pending EEOC sex discrimination lawsuit against Sears, Roebuck & Company. He said the lawsuit relies almost exclusively on statistics. A lawyer for Sears tried to get Thomas removed from his Chairmanship because of the statement. To be sure, it was a highly prejudicial comment for a lawyer to make who was involved in the litigation of the case.[lv]

Like a loose cannon, Thomas also, when the occasion arose, attacked Supreme Court decisions that applied to the Voting Rights Act and the Brown *v. Board of Education* decision in 1954. He objected to what he said was a presupposition by the Court that minorities would vote in blocs, and in the Brown case he found it illogical that the decision was based on the equal protection clause of the Fourteenth Amendment. He seemed to have a peculiar sense of constitutional law that others found difficult to understand.

In Clarence Thomas' war of words against the mission of the EEOC, he often put himself at odds with the Supreme Court, Congress and employers seeking to remedy past discrimination. "It is certainly appropriate for a private individual to hold and express such views, but when he expressed these views during the past decade, Thomas was not just a private individual. In 1981-2 he was Director of the Office of Civil Rights in the Department of Education, and from 1982 to 1988 he was Chair of the Equal Employment Opportunity Commission, and subsequently a judge of the U.S. Court of Appeals for the District of Columbia Circuit. In the former two positions, he was a public official sworn and paid to carry out certain civil-rights responsibilities under the law. The views he expressed in these, and other instances, were distinctly at odds with those responsibilities and thus tended to weaken the credibility of the public agencies he served. But, though offensive and improper, his expression of these views adverse to his public duty and oath of office is probably not a readily *impeachable offense* (emphasis mine), provided he duly carried out his public duty. But that is exactly what he did not do." [lvi]

The public record of Clarence Thomas at the EEOC was retrograde and dismal. He did not fulfill his public duty. He was chairman in name only at the EEOC with the undercover responsibility of sabotaging the mission of the agency, and he assumed this duty with great vigor. Time after time, he was dilatory, even defiant, in declining to do what the law, as embodied in statute, case law and court orders, required him to do.[lvii]

The Congressional Black Caucus was very familiar with the antics of Chairman Thomas at the EEOC, and the Caucus had this to say about him. "The Clarence Thomas record speaks for itself. It reflects a blind commitment to an ideology, which has caused him to misinterpret, misconstrue or ignore statutory laws with which he disagrees. He has revealed an allegiance to views about the fundamental rights embodied in our Constitution which are inimical to the interests of African Americans and the vast majority of the American public."[lviii]

The NAACP has been monitoring the operations of the EEOC since its earliest days, and the civil rights organization was appalled by the reversal of fortunes of the agency under Chairman Thomas. The NAACP noted that he revealed a hostility to constitutional principles effecting civil rights protections, including the use of meaningful remedies for both past and present discrimination such as "goals and timetables." Moreover, the longer he was in office the more antagonistic he became towards the mission of the EEOC. Once he had been confirmed for a second term, he dramatically increased his opposition to affirmative action. In fact, the NAACP found his positions so offensive and detrimental to the interests of African Americans, it called for his resignation at that time.[lix]

When President Reagan nominated Clarence Thomas for another four-year term in 1986, a number of organizations came forward to express objections, including civil rights organizations, the Black Leadership Forum, the National Women's Law Center, the National Women's Political Caucus, NOW Legal Defense Fund, the State Bar of Texas, and the American Federation of Government Employees.[lx]

Given the widespread opposition and the fact that Thomas' administrative record was as dilatory and harmful to the public interest as it has been described here, it should be asked why was he confirmed for a second term? After all, Reagan, conservative Republicans did not control the U.S. Senate, which was responsible for the confirmation. However, the truth of the matter is, confirmations of appointments to the Executive Branch are normally not based on merit. There is the ongoing political understanding between Democrats and Republicans that the President should have the individuals he wants to work for him. With exception of appointments to the judiciary, confirmations usually are pro forma exercises.

Also, Thomas' reconfirmation was for his leadership at the EEOC where he had opposed affirmative action policies and remedies, in particular quotas, and most of the members of the Senate were on the record as opposing quotas because quotas were supposedly used to deny equal employment opportunities to white male workers. And lest we forget, at the time, the Senate was 98% white males.

Keeping all this in mind, the most telling reason why Thomas was reconfirmed as head of the EEOC is still the fact that most of the federal government apparatus in Washington, D.C., regardless of the branch, is used to facilitate the politics, the policies, and the prejudices of the

President. In this regard, there is a very special relationship between the U.S. Senate and the Office of the Presidency. It is a relationship that the American people were warned about over two hundred years ago by the anti-federalists. They said then that the Senate and President looked too much like a King and a House of Lords, and that taken together, they equaled an oligarchy.

No doubt, the Office of the Presidency is very political and very powerful, and for some time now, pundits of the left and right have identified it as the *imperial presidency*. Indeed, my use in this essay of the Machiavellian characterization of *The Prince* is derived from this connotation. The Prince personifies the power, the politics, the ideology, and the arrogance of one who is President of the United States. Therefore, the Prince is not a person per se, but a name, a description that represents a list of attitudes and behaviors that can be attributed to, and exhibited by, the person in the White House.

When the poor boy from Pin Point, Georgia, Clarence Thomas, arrived in Washington, he was eager to serve his mentors. As a member of the Reagan Administration, and later the Bush Administration, he served his Prince. Probably, from this perspective, in his calculating mind, he thought of himself as having no public duty even though he served in a public office. He probably saw himself as working for the President.

With this attitude, Thomas committed himself to a program of administrative negligence and subversiveness that boggles the mind, and it led the *Leadership Conference on Civil Rights* to remark "…we believe that Clarence Thomas too often allowed his personal opinions to interfere with his constitutional and statutory responsibilities to enforce civil rights laws…He repeatedly and unilaterally decided to enforce those laws and court decisions with which he agreed and to ignore or deny those with which he disagreed. On too many occasions, (he) governed not by the rule of law, but by executive fiat." [lxi]

Finally, in this evaluation of the public record of Clarence Thomas at the EEOC, we should put to rest once and for all the idea that he was a person operating on his own, a bureaucratic rogue, *L' unique auteur* who got into the chicken house because someone made a mistake and left the door open. This view does not fit the image of the man who has descriptively materialized here.

In the world of his Prince, Thomas was an *OpporTOMist*. He, like all of us, lived in worlds within a world. He may have been master-like in his worlds at OCR and EEOC, but his lesser worlds were dependent upon the power in the over-world of the person in the White House. This being the case, it seems highly unlikely that he would have been rambunctious enough to attack the mission of the EEOC, the Supreme Court, and the U.S. Constitution without the approval of the Administration.

Moreover, the strategy to undermine civil rights enforcement was legalistic, complex, and defiant. In some instances, it called for acts of lawlessness. It is not likely that Clarence Thomas devise this strategy on his own. Logically, he must have had help from other members of the Reagan Administration, and he surely had the support of his Prince. More likely than not, there was probably a gaggle of conspirators involved in his underhanded activities; and make no mistake about it, Thomas did commit treasonous acts, by refusing to perform his constitutional duties and breaking faith with the American people. He betrayed the people's trust. But, what is even more outrageous is the fact that he received no punishment even though his guilt was publicly known. Instead, he was rewarded with a lifetime appointment to the United States Court of Appeals for the District of Columbia Circuit in February 1990.

As Judge of The Court of Appeals For The District of Columbia

By 1989, Clarence Thomas had become a "political hot potato" in the Bush Administration. His reckless administrative behavior had at last exposed him for what he was, an ideologue working for the success of the Reagan revolution. With his cover blown, it was not likely that he would be confirmed for a third term as Chairman of the EEOC. What then was to become of this dutiful soldier? The question was an empty one. For months, certain legal events had been preparing the next step for Thomas in government.

Thomas' appointment to the Court of Appeals was, in part, a reward for faithful service at two government agencies, but he may also have been elevated to the Court because he was needed to carry out another assignment for his mentors. No explanation needed. Any reward provided by the Prince is always on a *quid pro quo* basis. The nature of the assignment would materialize once he was seated on the Court.

But, there was opposition to overcome first. Thomas had made many enemies, in and out of government. The Prince would have to do some political arm-twisting, and he was especially motivated to do so in this case. As a member of the judiciary, Thomas would be put on ready alert. There was talk in official Washington that the black seat on the Supreme Court would be coming vacant soon.

Many different groups opposed Thomas' nomination to the federal bench, the most significant one being a group of congresspersons. When the word leaked out that President Bush was going to nominate Thomas to the Circuit Court of Appeals, fourteen members of the House wrote a letter to the President urging him not to do so. Their letter epitomizes the objections of the opposition to Thomas. Among the signatories, there were twelve chairpersons of committees, many of them having oversight responsibilities for the EEOC. These congresspersons were very well acquainted with the public service record of Clarence Thomas.

The letter to the President begins with the following statement: "We are writing to express concern about the possible nomination of Clarence Thomas to the U.S. Court of Appeals for the District of Columbia. Mr. Thomas' actions as chair of the Equal Employment Opportunity Commission raise serious questions about his judgment, respect for the law and general suitability to serve as a member of the Federal judiciary."

The congresspersons go on to say that when he was head of the EEOC, Thomas developed policy directives and enforcement strategies which undermined the effectiveness of the Age Discrimination In Employment Act and Title VII. In particular, his questionable enforcement record for Title VII of the 1964 Civil Rights Act frustrated the intent and purpose of the statute. Moreover, "the Chairman reportedly retaliated against an employee critical of the EEOC's enforcement of ADEA shortly after she presented testimony under subpoena from the Senate Committee (this is a violation of federal law and is currently under review).

The letter concludes with a very strong, damaging statement. "Mr. Thomas has demonstrated an overall disdain for the rule of law. For these reasons we believe he should not be nominated to the federal bench. His record as the EEOC Chair sends a clear message to those who have suffered job discrimination that he is insensitive to the injustice they have experienced. By nominating him, you will be reinforcing that message...We urge you not to nominate Clarence Thomas to the D.C. Circuit Court of Appeals."[lxii]

President Bush ignored the protest letter from the House, and Thomas was nominated and later confirmed. Once again, the Senate acquiesced to the desire of the Prince. In relationship to the President, the Senate tends to act like the British House of Lords.

Thomas was on the Court of Appeals for just sixteen months. During that time, he wrote only seventeen majority opinions for the Court. There is not much of a record here to evaluate, but if one takes an objective look at the written decisions of Judge Thomas, there are some definite clues to his judicial philosophy. *The Alliance For Justice* noted that there have been few dissents or separate concurrences of his opinions and in total his decisions do not overtly indicate an overall ideological tilt, although they are generally conservative.[lxiii]

In evaluating him as an Appeals Court Judge, the Congressional Black Caucus and the National Council of Churches of Christ in the USA, commented on his conservatism after reading all his opinions. The Caucus pointed out that during his brief period of service on the U.S. Court of Appeals, Thomas has repeatedly ruled against the accused in the face of alleged police or prosecutorial excesses. This suggests that he favors institutional rights of authority over individual, citizen rights.[lxiv]

The National Council of Churches of Christ found that Thomas' decisions, where appropriate, would limit access to the federal courts "…the tendency is already apparent in his brief tenure on the federal bench to also resort wherever possible to procedural rules in order to close the courthouse door against plaintiffs challenging governmental actions."[lxv]

Even though he had only a meager record as an appellate court judge, Thomas was still able to make a name for himself, as infamous as it turned out to be. In 1990, he wrote an opinion for the Court in violation of a federal statute that required him to disqualify himself on ethical grounds. Monroe Freedman, Howard Lictenstein Distinguished Professor of Legal Ethics at Hofstra University Law School, wrote about this case.

Professor Freedman states that the Judicial recusal statute, 28 U.S.C. 455, as amended in 1974, reads, 455(a), any federal judge "shall" disqualify himself in any proceeding in which the judge's impartiality "might" reasonably be questioned. The mandate of 455(a) was well established in

1990 when Judge Thomas sat in *Alpo Petfoods Inc. v. Ralston Purina Co.*, 913 F.2d958.

There was a nonparty in this case who had a definite interest in the outcome. This party was Senator John Danforth (R-Mo.). Judge Thomas had a personal relationship with Senator Danforth going back to 1974. It was Danforth who brought Thomas to Washington with him when he became a U.S. Senator, and it was Danforth who had personally helped Thomas become a member of the Reagan Administration.

Danforth had pushed Thomas along at each stop of his career ladder. "At each stage, Danforth testified publicly and effusively in Thomas' favor and lobbied for him behind the scenes. This sponsorship included Thomas' appointment to the federal appeals court, when Danforth described Thomas in testimony as his 'personal friend.'"

Senator Danforth also has close ties to the Ralston Purina Company. "The company was founded by the senator's grandfather, and members of the Danforth family remain major shareholders. The senator himself owns Ralston Purina stock worth more than $7.5 million. His brothers, William and Donald, are members of the company's board of directors and are also heavy holders of stock, and brother William is chancellor and a trustee of Washington University in St. Louis, which also has large holdings in Ralston Purina."

The case of *Alpo V. Ralston Purina* involved cross-charges of false advertising. "After a two-month bench trial, U.S. District Judge Stanley Sporkin found both companies in the wrong, but found that Ralston Purina alone had acted willfully. Indeed, he found that the firm had 'perpetrated a cruel hoax' on dog owners in its false claims that its dog food could cure a serious ailment. He therefore assessed a whopping $10.4 million penalty against Ralston Purina."

Judge Thomas had been on the Court bench for only a few weeks before the Ralston Purina appeal case was heard, "a case in which his patron's family was challenging not only a severe penalty but also a finding of deliberate dishonesty in its advertising." Moreover, why was the case being heard in the District of Columbia Circuit and not the Eighth Circuit Court of Appeals, which had U.S. District and appellate court jurisdiction for the state of Missouri? We can only guess at the reasons.

Should Judge Thomas have disqualified himself? On this matter of recusals, Supreme Court decisions have held that consistent with due process, judges should not only be unbiased, but also they must avoid even the appearance of bias. Certainly a reasonable person would have grounds to question Judge Thomas' impartiality, but he did not remove himself from the case.

Judge Thomas reversed the lower court, overturning the $10.4 million penalty against Ralston Purina and specifically disapproving the trial court's finding that Ralston Purina had perpetrated a "cruel hoax" by running advertisements that it knew lacked support. He wrote in his opinion that Ralston Purina's declarations of innocence could reflect "an honest difference of scientific opinion, rather than a specific intent to mislead consumers." Judge Thomas also found that Judge Sporkin's finding of bad faith on the company's part was "clearly erroneous."[lxvi]

By failing to recuse himself from the Ralston Purina case, was Judge Thomas in violation of federal law? Professor Freedman believes that the evidence strongly suggests that he was. And, very importantly, in writing his opinion, did Judge Thomas act out of bias for a friend? Did he declare innocence in the face of guilt? Was his mind already made up before he considered the evidence? And was he specifically recruited to sit as a judge on this case? We can't read minds. Therefore, we may never really know. But, we should remember that rewards from the Prince are only given on a *quid pro quo basis*.

Consider this: Judge Thomas' decision in this case was not simply a reversal of the lower court's findings. In the end, it amounted to a whitewash of all the charges against Ralston Purina, and let me say that that took some doing. For instance, Judge Thomas found that the penalty was proper only if there was a showing of bad faith or willfulness on the part of Ralston Purina. The fact that the company had no scientific data to support its advertising claims and the fact that the defendant tried to destroy documents relevant to the litigation did not amount to bad faith or willfulness, said Judge Thomas.

Too many pieces of this puzzle fit together perfectly. The ends, in this case, match so well with the means, it is difficult to believe that the situation developed coincidentally. We are asked to believe that Clarence Thomas just happened to be in the right place at the right time in order that he could use his official position to help a dear friend, who just happened to have been his professional mentor and sponsor for many years. It could have happened coincidentally, but that is highly unlikely.

To believe that there was no dishonesty in this case turns a sense of credulity into a quagmire. And, what does this say about Clarence Thomas? In just a brief period on the Appeals Court Bench, a matter of weeks, he had destroyed himself as a judge. For a person to be a judge, he must have the ability to be fair and impartial when adjudicating cases. Our entire legal system rests on the principle of judicial objectivity. Without it, there can be no rule of law, and no need for courts.

But, once again, Clarence Thomas demonstrated that he had a disdain for the *rule of law*, and more specifically, as a judge, he demonstrated a disdain for the fair and impartial administration of justice. In the Ralston Purina case, it appears as though Judge Thomas allowed himself to be used to serve the personal interest of a friend. He was used to secure and enhance the crass materialistic rewards of one of his mentors, who was a very close friend of the Prince, I should add. One wonders, if there was a *quid pro quo*, was it for the Senator or the President? In any event, as before, Judge Thomas had allowed himself to be used as a negative, social force against some aspect of the American legal and/or political system.

President Bush Nominates Clarence Thomas To Be An Associate Justice Of The Supreme Court

The Supreme Court is the Highest Court in America, with the primary responsibility for defending and interpreting the U.S. Constitution. This is probably the most powerful judicial body in the entire world. In our system of jurisprudence, it has the authority to override the will of the majority as expressed in an act of Congress, and it can forcefully remind a President that in this nation all persons are subject to the rule of law, as the Court did with President Nixon in the Watergate tapes matter. The Court can even require the redistribution of political power in every state in the union, and it can tell the American citizenry when it is time to change the fabric of the society, as was the case with the Brown desegregation decision in 1954.[lxvii]

Considering the social stature and political power of the Supreme Court, one might think that only the very best of the nation's jurists are elevated to this loftiest of court benches. Also, one might think that ideology and politics would be at a minimum in the selection process for justices. But history indicates just the opposite on both accounts.

As a social institution, the Supreme Court can have a tremendous influence on the conduct of social affairs in American society. Witness the Brown decision. For this reason, appointments to the Court have always been political, with much less concern for the judicial or intellectual merits of the justices.

Moreover, the Supreme Court is a powerful institution because, as a matter of law, it can uphold or deny existing social policy, and its decisions result as much from presuppositions as from interpretation of the law. The Court can be speculative in its decision-making, saying what *ought to be done,* based on a concept of fairness, and these views are unquestionably policy determinations based upon ideology.[lxviii] The focus of the Court's attention is not easily explainable by the use of *the rules of thumb* and *fundamental law.* Consequently, the Justices rely very heavily upon their own predilections, their sense of values, their subjective judgment, and their ideology.[lxix]

The principal power of the Court rests with judicial review. It was Chief Justice John Marshall who was mainly responsible for having the Court assume this enormous power. From the doctrine of judicial review has evolved the doctrine of judicial supremacy, and this is what gives the Court unequaled influence on the destiny of America. Ideology is important because it helps to shape the opinions and decisions of the Justices. Therefore, ideology is a determining factor in the choice of a nominee. It is a concern that moves the President to select a particular individual, and it is a concern that sways the Senate, one way or the other, in its confirmation hearings.[lxx]

There are nine Justices of the Supreme Court, but it takes only five members to finalize a decision. "The Ideology of one Justice, then, can change the outcome of an issue brought before that body. These Justices are humans, humans of widely varying abilities, backgrounds, and ideologies. And the Constitution is 'their letter of instruction.' How the Constitution will be read and interpreted by them will depend upon the ideological 'lens' through which they view the documents..."[lxxi]

A list of personal factors is always considered when a choice is being made for a seat on the Supreme Court. Age, sex, race, religion, physical and mental fitness, professional credentials, and even geography are noted, but ideology has usually been the overriding consideration. Over the years, there have been several broad ideological issues which have been used to evaluate Supreme Court nominees. The prominent issue today revolves around the political philosophies of judicial activism versus judicial restraint.

These labels of activism and self-restraint have been widely used to suggest the differences between Justices who are more willing to use their judicial powers to "correct" what they personally regard as "injustices" of laws and previous judicial decisions.[lxxii]

One of the items on the agenda of the Reagan revolution was that of completing the face lifting of the Supreme Court from a liberal to a more conservative body. The process had begun with President Nixon who took the first steps to change the "activist," liberal Court of Chief justice Earl Warren. Now in the Administration of George H. Bush, the process was almost complete. Conservative Justices were a majority on the Court. One more conservative, and a black conservative at that, would help to consolidate the majority's hold on that body.

In the third year of his Administration, on July 1, 1991, President George Bush nominated Judge Clarence Thomas to be an Associate Justice of the Supreme Court of the United States. Regardless of what the President said, the choice was made substantially on two counts: the candidate was black and he had the right conservative ideology. At the same time, the nomination also included a hidden agenda.

President Bush claimed that Judge Thomas was highly qualified to take the seat on the Supreme Court that had been left vacant by the retirement of Justice Thurgood Marshall. This certainly was not true, and if anything, he was highly unqualified. Consequently, there must have been other reasons why the President wanted him on the Court.

To begin with, another conservative on the Court would push that institution even further to the right. But, with a black conservative Justice, the Court could still maintain a sense of racial legitimacy in the eyes of the black community. Also, the Reagan revolution was moving government policy-making to the right. This movement disfavored the black community, and it would be the Court, which would be called upon to give legal legitimacy to these policy initiatives. A black on the Court would help to deflect some of the criticism from the liberal establishment. Therefore, Bush had nominated a black conservative to the Court for symbolic and political reasons.

Specifically, Clarence Thomas had been chosen because he was a black reactionary who would do the conservative movement's bidding without exception, and having a black man on the Court would neutralize attacks of racism brought against the Administration.[lxxiii] He was perfect for this role because throughout his professional career he had worked to conserve the political and economic status quo. Long ago, he had become a standard-bearer for the white-male elitist system that had spawned him, and at 43 he would be able to perform in this role for decades.[lxxiv]

With this particular nomination for the Supreme Court, Mr. Bush was indeed acting as Machiavelli's Prince. The Prince must assume that others, in government and society in general, are conspiring to take his power away from him. Therefore, he must use every means at his disposal to trick and deceive them. He believes that if his rivals were in power, they would do the same to him.

George Bush knew that many black Americans would support Thomas because he was black, and many liberals would support him for the same reason, regardless of his past public record. Any black was better than no black on the Supreme Court. And, Mr. Bush was also aware of the fact that many Democrats in the Senate would have difficulty voting against Mr. Thomas because they depended an the votes of black constituencies back in their states. To take advantage of this situation, in a very cynical gambit, Mr. Bush nominates an unqualified black conservative who would nullify the Democratic vote and split the civil rights community down the middle. Politically, it was a very shrewd move.[lxxv]

But, if you can believe it, President Bush was being even more cynical with the American people than first observation of this situation would indicate. In rejecting the liberalism of the past, the Reagan revolution was dividing America along racial lines. While at the same time, because of the theory of supply-side economics, the government, through tax breaks and the loosening of corporate regulations, was delivering more and more of the nation's resources to the richest among us. Because of the declining liberalism in government, the plight of the racial minorities and the poor were being ignored.[lxxvi]

Over time, various issues dealing with these resource distribution matters would be coming before the Court. The conservative movement did not want an "activist" Court that would use its judicial powers to correct social injustices. Moreover, from the probable thinking of the President, an unqualified black on the Supreme Court would not likely have a moral conversion and try to use his position to help his people.

Of course, President Bush did not take into consideration the character of Thomas' psychological profile. He was much more interested in the nominee's ideology.

AMERICAN BAR ASSOCIATION

The American Bar Association (ABA) is an organization composed of American lawyers and judges in voluntary association. It is a nongovernmental organization that seeks to promote improvements in the legal profession such as increased legal services to all citizens as needed, and an improved system in the administration of justice that would be more efficient and judicious.

Since 1948, the Senate Judiciary Committee has requested, and received, the opinion of the ABA's Standing Committee on Federal Judiciary on every federal judicial nomination. This routine has now developed into a tradition, and a person receiving an unfavorable opinion from the ABA is not likely to be confirmed by the Senate. To be sure, with an unfavorable opinion, it is more likely that the Attorney General of the United States would withdraw the nominee's name from consideration.

Two days after President Bush nominated Clarence Thomas for the Supreme Court, the ABA began its evaluation of his qualifications to sit on that High Bench. Given the shameful public record of the man, his lack of personal integrity, and his exhibitions of disdain for the *rule of law*, it would seem at the outset that he did not have the slightest chance of being approved as a candidate for the Supreme Court. But, to the disbelief of many, he was approved. For us to understand how this happened, we need to take a closer look at the ABA process.

Let us begin with the criteria used by ABA to evaluate all candidates to the federal courts. And, these criteria are placed at an even higher standard for nominees to the Supreme Court. The ABA directs its evaluation to professional qualifications, which include integrity, professional competence and judicial temperament.

The ABA holds that integrity is self-defining. However, a nominee's general reputation in the legal community, along with his or her industry and diligence, needs to be investigated. The organization also looks at professional competence from the point of view of intellectual capacity, judgment, writing and analytical ability, knowledge of the law and breadth or professional experience. As well, the ABA considers a nominee's compassion, decisiveness, open-mindedness, sensitivity, courtesy, patience, freedom from bias and commitment to equal justice. And finally, the health of the nominee is taken into account.

All of the above criteria are used to evaluate a candidate for the Supreme Court, but the ABA also believes that the Supreme Court requires a person with exceptional professional qualifications. "The significance, range and complexity of the issues considered by the Supreme Court, the importance at the underlying societal problems, the need to mediate between tradition and change and the Supreme Court's extraordinarily heavy docket are among the factors which require a person of exceptional ability."[lxxvii]

These were the evaluative criteria used by ABA to investigate Clarence Thomas for the Supreme Court, and he came through the investigation with a passing, if not a top rating, and on September 14, 1991, Ronald L. Olson, a practicing lawyer in Los Angeles, California and Chair of the Standing Committee on Federal Judiciary of the American Bar Association, sent a letter to the Honorable Joseph R. Biden, Jr., Chairman of the Committee an the Judiciary of the U.S. Senate, Re: *The Honorable Clarence Thomas*.

The letter, from one Chairman of a prestigious committee to another Chairman of a prestigious Committee, concerned itself with an evaluation of a third gentleman of a prestigious office who had been under the tutelage of two Presidents for ten years. The document was a report on the specific details of the investigation into the background of Clarence

Thomas. It goes on for some eight-plus pages and thoroughly explains itself rather well.

The report begins by proudly discussing the process used by the ABA committee members in the investigation. "Committee members interviewed over 1,000 persons throughout the United States, including well over 75 state and over 300 federal judges, 28 federal magistrate judges, and 29 federal bankruptcy judges. The interviews included present and former members of the Supreme Court of the United States, members of federal courts of appeals, members of the federal district courts, members of state courts, including those before whom Judge Thomas appeared as a practicing lawyer; and, in particular, Judge Thomas' colleagues from the United States Court of Appeals for the District of Columbia Circuit."[lxxviii]

This seems to have been a massive investigation. Why, even 300 practicing lawyers throughout the United States were questioned, and people from every stage of his professional life were interviewed, going back to his first job as a lawyer in the Office of the Attorney General of the State of Missouri. Additionally, over 150 deans and faculty members of law schools throughout the United States, including some 12 professors at the law school which Judge Thomas attended, and constitutional and Supreme Court scholars. And lastly, special reading committees reviewed all of Judge Thomas' opinions.

At first look, the work of the ABA seems very impressive, but on second look an obvious question comes to mind. Did the investigators speak to all the people who knew Judge Thomas all the time or did they just speak to some of the people who knew Judge Thomas only some of the time? To get a comprehensive picture of the nominee, it would have been necessary to speak to friend and foe alike. This does not seem to have been done.

For instance, the report says that the ABA people spoke to persons who had worked with Judge Thomas at the Department of Education and the EEOC, but apparently no one mentioned that while he was at OCR he frequently refused to carry out his duties under the law, an act of nonfeasance to be sure, and behavior that was reprehensible in a public administrator, but entirely unacceptable for a Supreme Court Justice. And certainly, no investigator spoke with Judge John H. Pratt on the matter of Assistant Secretary Thomas refusing to carry out a court order from the Adams case. A person who has no respect for the law is not morally suited to be a judge at any level of our judicial system.

If there had been a thorough investigation of Chairman Thomas' record at the EEOC, surely the nature of his misfeasance and malfeasance administrative behavior would have come to light. By opposing affirmative action remedies, he knowingly sabotaged the mission of an agency that was under his responsibility. Furthermore, it was an incredible act of omission for the ABA investigators not to speak to the fourteen members of Congress who pleaded with the President not to nominate Clarence Thomas to the Appeal's Court Bench because "he has demonstrated an overall disdain for the rule of law." Maybe they did speak to these House members, but if they did, then they rationalized the objections to Thomas or the objections were ignored altogether.

A Supreme Court Justice is expected to be sensitive and have compassion for others. At the EEOC, Chairman Thomas exhibited just the opposite type of human character. He refused to protect the employment rights of older workers, and he neglected to rescind regulations that cost them more than $1.5 billion in retirement income. Under his direction, the EEOC failed to process discrimination claims by older workers before the statute of limitations ran out. Thousands upon thousands of such workers were unable to pursue their claims in court. How could all of this have been overlooked?

The report does say "a few interviewees expressed disagreement with Judge Thomas' interpretation of equal employment laws at the EEOC and his failure to adhere to existing court orders. These disagreements raised doubts as to his professional integrity. However, the report goes on to say that "the Committee investigated these concerns and is satisfied that the disagreement over the interpretation of the law reflects an honest and reasonable difference of opinion."

What nonsense. Chairman Thomas' failure to look after the employment rights of older workers had nothing to do with interpretations of the law. It had to do with willful, administrative negligence. If the ABA people had spoken to the Chairs of the oversight House Committees, they would have found this out.

Nevertheless, nothing shames the ABA investigative Committee more than its failure to consider Judge Thomas' involvement in the Ralston Purina case of his friend and mentor, Senator John Danforth. This matter spoke to all the principal concerns of the investigative Committee. Judge Thomas found himself in a conflict of interest situation, and he refused to withdraw from the case putting him in violation of federal law. As professor Monroe Freedman said, in writing about Thomas and the Ralston Purina case, because the nominee failed to recuse himself he is not fit to sit on the Supreme Court.

Members of the investigation team certainly knew about Thomas and his involvement with the Ralston Purina case. Special reading committees read all of his judicial opinions. But, even reading committees raised no questions, Professor Freedman's article was published in the *Legal Times*, and he certainly raised questions about Judge Thomas' ethics. As lawyers, reviewing the ethics of a lawyer, this should have been the most damaging of evidence.

After one of its investigations of a nominee to the federal bench, the ABA will issue one or three ratings: well qualified, qualified, or not qualified. Judge Thomas received a *qualified*, and as a consequence this tells us one thing for certain. Lawyers, like doctors, are very protective of their own. But there is more to this favoritism for Judge Thomas than colleague cronyism.

It had been only a year and a half earlier that this same ABA had given its qualified approval to Clarence Thomas to be judge of the Appellate Court in the District of Columbia Circuit. That earlier approval was only one step removed from the Supreme Court. How could the ABA change its mind about him now without casting doubt and discredit on their earlier evaluation, and if the earlier evaluation was discredited, it would invalidate the latter one.

Could it also have been that the Prince planned this trap for the ABA? It is a definite possibility. Once Clarence Thomas had been approved for the Appellate Court, the ABA was already committed to approving him for the Supreme Court, particularly if the second nomination came close on the heels of the first. For the sake of its own good name, in organizational terms, Judge Thomas was going to be approved regardless of his qualifications.

There is also an aesthetic character to the ABA process. Truth is in the eye of the beholder. The ABA recognizes itself as a prestigious organization, and in this instance it was doing a job for the most prestigious office in the land, the office of the President of the United States. It is presumed that the President is an honorable man, and therefore his nominee for the Supreme Court would also have to be an honorable man of high moral character. If it were otherwise, the President would not have chosen him. However, this reductionism may be wrong, and if so it sets up a false premise. The President may not be an honorable man.

In any case, let us assume that the ABA did conduct its investigation based on the premise that the President was an honorable man. To verify the fact that one honorable man had chosen another honorable man for the Court, the ABA was likely to use its investigation to accent the positive while eliminating the negative. There would be little consideration for the middle ground. All negative findings will be seen in a positive light, and the benefit of the doubt is always given to the candidate.

In the end, it can be said that the ABA did a *no-job,* or was it a *snow job,* with the investigation of Clarence Thomas for the Supreme Court. At the same time, we have to consider the fact that the hand of the Prince stretches very far, very, very far.

SENATE JUDICIARY COMMITTEE

The U.S. Senate must confirm every federal judicial nomination, but before going to the floor for a full Senate vote, the nominee must face the Judiciary Committee of the Senate for a full round of confirmation hearings. In fact, usually confirmation is either gained or lost in the Committee before the full Senate takes up the matter. A Committee vote, up or down, tells the Senate whether the nominee has been found acceptable or not, and it is therefore a guide to the membership of the full body.

In recent years, the Judiciary Committee has become a battleground for ideologies and causes from the left and right of the political spectrum. Nominees to the Supreme Court have had to measure up to one or the other profile, liberal or conservative. These postures have become extremely important for the Court. Since the days of the Civil Rights Movement, the political mainstream of America has been moving to the right. President Nixon nurtured the "silent majority" to begin the trend.

Since the 1950s, the liberal court of Chief Justice Earl Warren had supported political gains on the left. However, appointments to the Court by a series of conservative, Republican Presidents eliminated the liberal majority. Nevertheless, the liberal establishment still looked to the Court to preserve its social and political gains that were becoming increasingly under attack as a consequence of conservative government policies and a more conservative judiciary.

With the nomination of Robert H. Bork for the Supreme Court in1987, the ideological litmus test for a nominee was his stand on the constitutional rights of *personal liberty*. It had become a matter of debate because of the 1973 Supreme Court decision in the Roe v. Wade case, which granted women the right to an abortion. The issue of a woman's right to an abortion had split the nation politically, pro and con, and the Senators, on and off the Committee, had been similarly affected. Liberals tended to support abortion rights; while conservatives tended to oppose it. A Conservative Supreme Court could overturn the Roe decision.

During his confirmation hearings, Clarence Thomas was sure to be asked to state his position on Roe and a woman's right to an abortion. Prior to the start of the hearings, his exact position on the issue was unknown, but that would have to be cleared up because pro-abortion rights groups, with allies on the Judiciary Committee, wanted to use the Committee as a defense, a bulwark against attempts to overturn Roe. Robert Bork made it clear that he thought Roe was a bad precedent to use to permit abortions, and he was voted down by the committee and not confirmed by the Senate.

The abortion issue was expected to be divisive because the Judiciary Committee contained party and ideological factions. There were hard-core liberals and hard core conservatives, and a few moderates sprinkled in between. The liberals tended to be Democrats and the conservatives tended to be Republicans. The Democrats had the numbers. Their party controlled the Senate and that gave them control of the Judiciary Committee. By party, there were eight Democrats and six Republicans.

As the Thomas hearings began, this is the way the members of the Committee lined up. For the Democrats, Joseph R. Biden, Jr., from Delaware, was Chairman. He was a strong defender of the Roe V. Wade decision, but he had given no public indication on how he might vote in the Thomas matter. Edward M. Kennedy, Massachusetts, was a strong supporter of abortion rights, but he had been quiet on the Thomas nomination.

Howard M. Metzenbaum, Ohio, was likely to be Thomas' chief antagonist. He was expected to question the nominee on his record of enforcing age-discrimination laws at the EEOC. Metzenbaum was the only member of the judiciary Committee that voted against Thomas' confirmation to the Court of Appeals.

Dennis DeConcini, Arizona, had doubts about Judge Thomas' belief in a philosophy of "natural law" that ranged above the allocation of constitutional rights. He said he wanted Thomas to dispel any notion that he was a "radical conservative." Patrick J. Leahy, Vermont, said he had made no decision on Thomas, but he did have some questions about his views on personal liberties. Howell Hefflin, Alabama, was taking his traditional wait-and-see attitude toward judicial nominees.

Paul Simon, Illinois, had not announced how he would vote on the Thomas nomination, but he had been in the forefront of critics who suggested that Judge Thomas failed to enforce the law during his tenure as head of the EEOC. Lastly, Herb Kohl, Wisconsin, was undecided about whether to support Judge Thomas. He said he was not leaning one way or the other. However, he was interested in Thomas' views on the right to privacy.

For the Republicans, Strom Thurmond, South Carolina, was the ranking Republican on the Committee and an ardent and vocal supporter of Judge Thomas. He had defended Thomas' actions as head of the EEOC, and he had dismissed calls for Thomas to disclose how he would rule on controversial issues like abortion. Orrin G. Hatch, Utah, was forthright behind Thomas, and he would be making the White House's case on behalf of the nominee. Hatch had been a good friend of Thomas for many years.

Alan K. Simpson, Wyoming, was known to be the most sharp-tongued and aggressive of the Committee's Republicans. It was believed that he would be Judge Thomas' protector if Thomas came under attack. He would attack the attackers, something he was known to be very good at doing. As well, he admired Thomas because he believed that the Judge was on the cutting edge of black conservatism.

Arlen Specter, Pennsylvania, was a moderate, non-aggressive, partisan Republican. His opposition to Judge Bork had ensured Bork's defeat. But he was best known for devising the "single bullet" theory of the Warren Commission's investigation into the assassination of John F. Kennedy. He was uncommitted on the Thomas nomination, but he had said that the Committee had a duty to put Thomas under a microscope.

Charles E. Grassley, Iowa, had a reputation for being a reliable supporter of the Bush Administration nominees. He would criticize other members of the Committee who might try to make Thomas' confirmation subject to a "litmus test" on issues, and he has said that Thomas should not be criticized for opposing affirmative action. And finally there was Hank Brown, Colorado, a freshman in the Senate. He said he was impressed with Thomas' background, but he was withholding a decision until after the hearing.[lxxix]

These were the man on the Judiciary Committee that Clarence Thomas would have to face, and get their approval, in order to become politically the most powerful black person in the United States. The American people were undecided about his fate. On the morning of the first day of the hearings, September 10, 1991, the New York Times reported that a New York Times/CBS News Poll found that most American were undecided on the Thomas nomination, and this was equally the case for blacks or whites.

Aside from the polls, Thomas was the odds-on favorite to win approval if he did not expose himself as a black, right wing ideologue, which is exactly what he was, because the liberal members of the Committee did not fancy voting against a black man who had worked his way up from poverty during a time of white supremacy in the South. But, if he appeared to be a radical conservative, a crypto-fascist, as many liberals believed Robert Bork to be, then he would have to taste defeat, regardless of the impact on the black community.

Ignoring the sympathy and empathy track, the New York Times in an editorial called for a wide-ranging, comprehensive look at the nominee. The paper based its call on the fact that the Senate had a constitutional role to be a full partner in the appointment process, and it went on to say that "contrary to theories that the Senate's 'advice and consent' role is limited to measuring a nominee's technical fitness, the confirmation power is as broad as the President's power to nominate. No less then the chief executive, the Senators can weigh policy and ideology."[lxxx]

The paper listed some key areas that should be explored by the Committee: Thomas' legal qualifications, family background, his attitude on civil rights, natural law, personal liberty, and the nature of his conservative ideology.

It was Senator John C. Danforth, Thomas' sponsor, who officially opened the hearings by introducing him to the Senate Judiciary Committee. Senator Danforth went on to make a series of praiseworthy and laudatory remarks, and saying that the Clarence Thomas he knew would *be an extraordinary justice on the Supreme Court.* Given the personal and professional relationship that had existed between these two men, one might expect this kind of statement from the Senator, which was nothing more than greasing the wheels of the Committee. His introductory remarks set the stage for a Committee hearing performance that was nothing more than a game of 'hide-and-go-seek,' with much more hide than seek.

Thomas, the President, Senator Danforth, and all of the nominee's mentors knew that he could not present himself to the Committee as the black Reagan, right wing saboteur that got him the nomination. He had to present himself as something other than what he was, and he would be better off if he could present no self at all. It is difficult enough to hit a moving target, but it is practically impossible to hit the target if you don't know what you're shooting at.

Over the summer, from the time of the nomination to the day of the hearing, Thomas and his White House handlers developed a strategy for the Committee. It was the following: When being questioned by opponents on the Committee, with the help of the Republican membership, the nominee would hide in plain view while making reference to, and reaping the psychic and emotional benefits of, his poverty to prominence background.

It was Thomas' plan not to have an opinion on any controversial issue. He was to give an intellectual "soft shoe dance" to any penetrating questions that probed his political and/or judicial philosophy. If the Committee wanted to get at his real beliefs on such matters, they were not going to get him to articulate them.

The real Clarence Thomas never arrived at the Judiciary Committee hearings. "When pressed on matters of the moment, he backed away from almost every opinion he had ever expressed. Incredibly, he told Senators with a straight face that he had 'no opinion on Roe v. Wade, thus marking himself as probably the only person in the U.S. without a view on the Supreme Court's land mark abortion-rights decision. 'Thomas' answers and explanations about previous speeches, articles and positions' said Alabama Senator Howell Heflin, 'raised thoughts of inconsistencies, ambiguities, contradictions, lack of scholarship, lack of convictions and instability.'"[lxxxi]

In fact, what the nominee did was refuse to answer questions because he knew that the liberal Senators on the Committee were in a very tough bind. Since President Bush nominated Thomas, discussions about him always included race. The general thinking was: to be for Thomas was to be for blacks; to oppose Thomas was to be against blacks in the manner of the neo-nazi David Duke. In private, Democrats on the Committee were reluctant about pressing the nominee in any way that might bring up a confrontation on race, which validated Mr. Bush's political judgment that a black candidate would present a difficult target for opponents.[lxxxii]

Thomas had even stronger restricting fingers around the throat of the liberal faction of the Committee. All the members of the Committee were white, and the Democrats who controlled the Committee had no desire to conduct a debate on whether there is more than one legitimate ethnic ethos among blacks in America.[lxxxiii] That would be like taking a tiger by the tail, and at the moment the Democrats were comfortable playing pussycat.

Indeed, Thomas and his handlers had decided to play charades with the hearings. There would be questions asked, but no clear answers given. And the intimidated Democrats went along with the game. Their performance infuriated the liberal community, but the Democrats on the Committee found themselves caught in a trap set by the Prince. And they were not alone. Republican Senators who were not members of the Judiciary Committee were saying privately that they could read the polls with the best of them, and the polls were saying that a lot of black folks were for Thomas. Almost all of the Republican Senators had sizable black constituents, and they would be afraid to vote against a black nominee, especially when the President was demanding party loyalty.

Starting with the Judiciary Committee, there was an ideological battle being nurtured in the Senate for the sole purpose of divide and conquer. In Machiavellian terms, these types of ideological face-offs help to keep lieutenants, sundry party members, and opponents in government off balance and sniping at one another. The people who work with, and for, the Prince must be set against each other and maneuvered into impotence.[lxxxiv] It is a matter of political survival. People who work close with the Prince must be rendered safe.

But, this manipulation of subordinates and opponents encourages strained relations between them, and it makes it much more difficult for them to function cooperatively, to listen to one another, to formulate compromise, to coalesce politically. It is that government by innuendo again, and it was causing the Senators to feel under pressure from forces they could not control. One can genuflect to Prince and party but so many times; then the knees begin to hurt. Because of the Thomas confirmation hearings, both Democrats and Republicans in the Senate were hurting.

The ideological struggle that was going on was indicative of the political reality of official Washington. Divisiveness was important to a conservative style of governance, and Presidents Reagan and Bush spent a great deal of their time fighting coalescence in government. Perhaps this was because the conservatives were trying to weed out liberalism; or maybe there was a more fundamental reason than that. This divisiveness may be due to the fallacy that you can have right wing politics, with its hidden agendas, in a democratic form of government.

With the Thomas nomination, President Bush cynically and calculatingly set up a situation that would produce a divisive ideological battle in the Senate and throughout the nation. David Broder, a respected Washington newspaper columnist, reported that after Thomas' nomination had been decided, this instance of the politics of divisiveness had been planned in the White House back in 1990. In the previous year, President Bush had appointed David H. Souter to the Supreme Court. Souter was called the "stealth" nominee because so little was known about him, and Bush had purposely chosen him because he did not want an ideological fight over his appointee at that time.

When Souter was picked in the summer of 1990, Bush was in the middle of budget negotiations with Congress. His no-new-taxes pledge that had helped him get elected had been abandoned. "He needed to get something in return. 'And the venom of an ideological battle over a Supreme Court nomination would inevitably poison the chances of the budget summit accomplishing its objective.'"

"In addition," says Broder. "Bush did not want to heighten the visibility of the abortion issue at a time when several abortion-rights Republicans, including the GOP gubernatorial candidates in such key states as California and Illinois, were about to face the voters."

However, 1991 would be a different year, with a different set of circumstances, and should the opportunity for another appointment to the Court arise, "Bush might well find it useful then to nail down his conservative base by making a more ideological appointment," said Broder.

Broder claimed that he got his information from several very senior White House officials, and they gave him the name of three federal judges who could possibly be one or more ideological appointees in 1991. One of the names of the three was that of Judge Clarence Thomas. The thinking from the White House went like this: "If Thurgood Marshall were the retiree, how would Democrats feel about blocking Judge Thomas and making the court all-white again?"

Speaking of the plan at the Bush White House, to go ideological with the next appointment, Broder says, "Such considerations may strike you as cynical. But they are a good deal more honest than President Bush's pretense that he searched the country for the best possible nominee and was surprised and delighted to find that it just happened to be a black conservative named Thomas."[lxxxv]

Well, so much for the qualifications of Clarence Thomas for the Supreme Court. In the White House selection process, it was never a consideration. The President made perfunctory remarks, and Thomas acted the part of a phony. Bush willfully used him once again as a negative force, and Thomas didn't care that he was being so treated. To be sure, the entire public presentation of Thomas was nothing more than a sham.

Sham or no sham, the President wanted his black nominee on the Supreme Court, and despite Thomas' know-nothing, amorphous, invisible man testimony, and the fact that more than 50 national organizations opposed his nomination, including the NAACP, A.F.L.-C.I.O., The United Auto Workers, the National Education Association, the National Organization for Women, the National Abortion Rights Action League and the Mexican American League and Education Fund, Clarence Thomas still managed to squeak through the Committee.

The Committee vote on Clarence Thomas was seven to seven, and with the exception of the Democrat from Arizona, Dennis DiConcini, the vote was along party lines. Senator DiConcini had a special reason for voting with the Republicans, and that reason would be stressed even more in the next episode of the Thomas confirmation hearings. The vote notwithstanding, the hearings would not yet come to an end because in the immortal words of Yogi Berra, "It ain't over until it's over."

With a seven to seven vote from the Committee, Thomas was in a good position for full Senate confirmation, but even as the vote was being taken, an unexpected challenge was about to confront Thomas, the President, the U.S. Senate, and in particular the Judiciary Committee, on the way to the Supreme Court.

THE SEXUAL HARASSMENT CHARGE

Clarence Thomas had sat before the Judiciary Committee for five days, dodging questions of substances like a prizefighter avoiding punches in a boxing ring. He was so skillful, the full Committee hardly laid a glove on him, and with a seven to seven vote which means no recommendation, up or down, to the full Senate, the President was surely going to get him over the last hurdle.

Then, on the eve of the full Senate vote, the Long Island newspaper *Newsday* and National Public Radio reported that a woman had informed the Committee that she had been sexually harassed by Thomas when they worked together at the Department of Education and the EEOC in the early 1980s. The Republicans thought that opponents of Clarence Thomas had leaked the FBI report of the woman's statement at the last minute in a final attempt to block his confirmation.

But, the nomination had left the Committee, been reported to the Senate floor, and had been scheduled for a vote before the sexual harassment allegation had surfaced. The Republican leadership of the Senate, with the backing of the White House, did not want to postpone the vote, but all concerned realized that this was a very serious charge directed at a Supreme Court nominee. What could, or what should be done?

As the White House and the Senate leadership pondered over what to do, more and more information about the harassment allegation was hitting the news wires. The woman making the charge, Anita Hill, was now a professor at the University of Oklahoma Law School. She claimed that

Thomas had made suggestive remarks to her and urged her to go out on dates with him. She did not mention any physical abuse.

Within hours of the leak to the press, opponents of the Thomas nomination began to call for a reopening of the hearings to investigate the charge against him. This was something the Senate was reluctant to do because the President wanted the vote to proceed as soon as possible, but also because it went against Senate tradition if not Senate procedural rules. With a delay, there was the further possibility that something new might turn up to besmirch the already tarnished image of the nominee, and this is exactly what the liberal community was hoping and praying for.

The call for a postponement turned itself into a demand when it became known that the Judiciary Committee knew about the sexual harassment charge before it voted on Thomas, and it was assumed that the Committee had not taken the allegation seriously. Women's groups around the country were suddenly up in arms. The all-male Judiciary Committee had shown an extraordinary insensitivity to women by disregarding the charge of sexual harassment; and now that the negligence of the Committee was known, correcting its mistake was a matter for the full Senate. Moreover, spokeswomen across the country let the Senators and the President know that if they tried to ignore this matter, they would be remembered when the next election came around.

For Thomas and his supporters, matters had quickly gone from bad to worse. To be confirmed to the Supreme Court, only a simple majority was necessary, but the Republicans on their own did not have the margin for victory. They needed the votes of Democrats. The Senate was made up of 55 Democrats and 45 Republicans. At least five Democrats would have to vote for Thomas. If there were a tie Senate vote, Vice-President J. Danforth Quayle would break it in a vote for Thomas. The Republicans were counting on the Southern Democratic Senators who had large black constituencies to vote for Thomas, certainly the two Democratic Senators from Thomas' home state of Georgia.

Feeling the pressure, the Republican leadership took a head count and realized that the votes to confirm Thomas were no longer there. The harassment allegation had caused some Senators to reevaluate their support for the nominee, and the White House was informed. Shortly thereafter, Clarence Thomas asked for a delay on the Senate vote. He said he wanted the opportunity to clear his name, but in truth it was the lack of votes and public pressure, from hordes of radical feminists, said one conservative newspaper columnist, forced the request for the delay.

Stepping back from its rules and tradition, the leaders of the Senate agreed to a postponement. The confirmation vote was put off for one week, and the Judiciary Committee was told to hear Professor Hill's testimony, along with any other person's testimony that had a bearing on this matter. Of course, Judge Thomas would be given the opportunity to reply to the charges.

Subpoenas had to be prepared and issued from the Judiciary Committee. A schedule of witnesses had to be determined, and this took days, more time than what one would think under the circumstances. In fact, the Republicans were trying to use up the time on procedural matters to limit the number of witnesses who wanted to testify against Thomas. The ploy worked. By the time the second set of hearings began, there were only four days left before the next scheduled confirmation vote. Given the fact that a report had to be prepared and distributed to the other members of the Senate before the vote could take place, two or three days at the most was not enough time to really explore this most damaging and serious issue.

To be sure, the Senate, its Judiciary Committee, Thomas and his supporters did not want to explore this issue in any more detail then was absolutely necessary. Members of the news media were saying that the entire Senate was on trial over this harassment allegation, and the institution was going to be hard pressed to redeem itself. However, during the interim, new allegations were coming to light that were putting Thomas and his supporters even more on the defensive. Nevertheless, the process had to go forward.

To counter their defensive posture, the Republicans exploded with a media blitz over the leak of Anita Hill's FBI report, which was inaccurate. It was not her FBI report that had been leaked, but her statement to Committee staffers. All the same, the Republicans went on saying it was the FBI report, and this constituted a criminal offense, implying that an illegality can produce no good. The Democrats on the Committee all claimed innocence and wished the finger of blame on someone else. With the leak issue, the Republicans were raising a tempest in a teapot problem. Leaks were all too common in the Senate, and in that regard the leak of the Hill affidavit was no different than hundreds of other such leaks. It was just that the *unlawful* theme played very well with conservative constituents. All the same, the issue of the leak did cause the Democrats to refrain from commenting on the sexual harassment charge against Thomas. This gave the Republicans practically free reign of the airwaves on the subject. As matters progressed, the Republicans on the Committee would be able to say whatever they wanted about Anita Hill, with little rebuttal from the Democrats.

With Senator Biden smarting from accusations that he was chiefly responsible for the Committee's failure to give serious consideration to Anita Hill's charge, the second round of hearings began before a crowded hearing room of TV cameras and news people. The nation was now tuned into the Thomas Supreme Court process. Biden gave an opening guideline commentary in which he essentially said that the proceedings were not to be conducted like a hearing in a court. Translated, this meant, "Anita," who was already seated at the witness table, "it will be your word against his." And with that, Biden and his fellow Democrats settled back in their seats and turned the hearings over to the Republican minority on the Committee.

As Professor Anita Hill introduced herself to the Committee, there was no doubt that most of the Senators would have preferred to deal with this sticky situation in closed session, but the American people had now become a direct party to the proceedings. The television camera would be their interested, probing eye for the next three days in that Committee room, and what a three days it was.

The media described the event as theatre of the absurd, a seedy drama, a TV circus, an ugly sideshow, a pornographic show and tell; and as I would put it, the face-off between Anita Hill and Clarence Thomas was a bizarre attempt to raise humiliation to the level of respectability. The Committee began an investigation into allegations of a very sordid matter, and before the inquiry was over the Committee had become the sordid object of the investigation.

In a very controlled, none emotional style, Hill testified before the Committee. She told the members, and the American people, that during the time she worked with Clarence Thomas at the Department of Education and the EEOC, he had pestered her for dates and discussed explicit sexual matters with her. When he first asked that they see each other socially, she said, "I declined the invitation to go out socially with him, and explained to him that I thought it would jeopardize...a very good working relationship...I believed then, as now, that having a social relationship with a person who was supervising my work would be ill advised. I was very uncomfortable with the idea and told him so."

She thought that would end the matter, but it did not, "...to my regret, in the following few weeks, he continued to ask me out on several occasions...these incidents took place in his office, or mine. They were in the form of private conversations, which would not have been overheard by anyone else."

At some point, her working relationship with Thomas became even more strained when he began using work situations to discuss sex, and sometimes these discussions would take place in the government cafeteria. "After a brief discussion of work, he would turn the conversation to a discussion of sexual matters. His conversations were very vivid. He spoke about acts that he had seen in pornographic films involving such matters as women having sex with animals, and films showing group sex or rape scenes.

"He talked about pornographic materials depicting individuals with large penises or large breasts involving various sex acts.

"On several occasions, Thomas told me graphically of his own sexual prowess."

When these discussions would come up, she said she would try to change the subject, but her efforts were rarely successful. After a time, these encounters did stop for a while, just before Thomas moved to the EEOC. She thought his sexual improprieties had stopped altogether and that is why she accompanied him to the EEOC. She wanted to work in the civil rights field, and being at the EEOC was the best place to be for this type of work.

But at the EEOC, the harassment began again, and when she continued to reject his responses, he began to show certain displeasure with her. Still, he continued to make these unwanted advances. Hill said, "One of the oddest episodes I remember was an occasion in which Thomas was drinking a Coke in his office. He got up from the table at which we were working, went over to his desk to get the coke, looked at the can and asked, 'Who has put pubic hair on my coke?'"

"On other occasions, he referred to the size of his own penis as being larger than normal and he also spoke on some occasions of the pleasures he had given to women with oral sex. At this point, late1982, I began to feel severe stress on the job. I began to be concerned that Clarence Thomas might take out his anger with me by degrading me or not giving me important assignments. I also thought that he might find an excuse for dismissing me."[lxxxvi]

Members of the Judiciary Committee listened to these graphic sexual details, from this demure, calm black woman, and they were visibly embarrassed and shaken. Such obscenities in the venerated halls of Congress over an issue that the majority of the Senators did not take seriously (most of the Senators admitted that they thought sexual harassment

John L. Cooper, Ph.D. • 61

had to include some type of physical abuse, touching), and this was a black woman accusing a black man on national television. What an unheard of spectacle for official Washington.

This was seamy, sordid stuff, and it was washing right over the Senate Judiciary Committee, if not the entire Senate. If this women's accusations were true, how did this man ever manage to reach such high office, and now was being considered for an even higher place in officialdom. The American people were watching and wondering. The Senate was on the spot. The judgment of the institution was in question. The Senate had confirmed Clarence Thomas three previous times. The woman, for the good name of the Senate, had to be wrong, but maybe she wasn't.

The tide of public opinion was already flowing heavily against the members of the Judiciary Committee. The members were feeling the sting from feminist groups across the nation. The women were saying that the all-male body of the Committee, if not the entire Senate, except two, *just didn't get it*. They were inclined not to take sexual harassment seriously. The radical feminists were saying that the Senate had dropped the ball once. If they drop it twice, they would have to pay double indemnity in the next election.

It was a no win situation for the Democratic Senators on the Committee, and they wanted to get out of the glare of the sexual harassment spotlight without making anymore-political mistakes. If they were to get such relief, it would not come directly from them because in the eyes of television it could not appear as though they were shirking their duty. Under the circumstances, the best possible person to give them relief would be Clarence Thomas in the manner of his defense, and on cue, he delivered.

If Thomas and his supporters, especially President Bush, knew that liberal Democrats were unwilling to antagonize him with tough questions because of his race, they certainly knew that those same Democrats would not interrogate him over an allegation of sexual harassment from a black woman. Besides, the Democrats were not thinking that deeply. They were looking for a covert way to concede, and Thomas gave it to them.

When Thomas sat at the witness table, it was evening, prime television time, and he took center stage. The schedule of witnesses had been set up purposefully in this way. Hill would have the day and Thomas would have the night. More people watch television in the evenings, and the President wanted Thomas to get maximum TV exposure so that his side of the story could be heard by as many of the American people as possible. It was obvious that the Republicans were manipulating the situation in whatever way they could.

Thomas began his testimony with a prepared statement, delivering it in a very cool, calm, but forceful manner. He could have been trying to counter the image of Anita Hill, composed and dignified, with a similar image of himself. He categorically denied all the charges made by Hill, and then he proceeded to outline the working relationship they had had together, as he remembered it. The summation of his overall statement was that nothing of a personal, social, sexual improper nature occurred. Hill and he had had a good working relationship and that was all of it.

But, as he came to the end of his prepared statement, his voice became stronger, more resonant and angry. "Mr. Chairman, I am a victim of this process. My name has been harmed. My integrity has been harmed. My family has been harmed. My friends have been harmed. There is nothing this committee, this body, or this country can do to give me my good name back. Nothing."

"I will not provide the rope for my own lynching, or for further humiliation. I am not going to engage in discussions, nor will I submit to roving questions, of what goes on in the most intimate parts of my private life, or the sanctity of my bedroom. These are the most intimate parts of my privacy, and they will remain just that: private."

After his statement, as Professor Hill had done, he submitted to questions from the panel. He took the line of the injured party, and he refused to discuss any of the details of the relationship he had with Anita Hill when they worked together. He wouldn't even discuss her testimony as he told an astonished Judiciary Committee that he had not watched her on TV earlier in the day.

In fact, what Clarence Thomas now did was to attack the Judiciary Committee and the nomination process. With anger in his voice, he invoked racial imagery that had not been used previously in the hearings. He denounced the Committee's handling of the Hill allegations, accusing the Committee of tactics that went far beyond McCarthyism. He said the panel was ruining the country and ruining him. He said that black men who did not "kowtow to an old order" would "be lynched, destroyed, caricatured by a Committee of the U.S. Senate rather than hung from a tree…" He compared his ordeal to a "high-tech lynching, for uppity blacks."

Whatever the gain for Thomas in attacking the Committee and the process, it seemed strange for those who knew his record to hear him fall back an the images of the civil rights movement to make his case. When he was Chairman of the EEOC, he became an increasingly fervent spokesman against the approaches of the traditional civil rights groups. "As his relations with those groups worsened, he complained in an interview with The Washington Post in 1984 that all the nation's traditional civil rights leaders do is, 'bitch, bitch, bitch, moan and whine.'"[lxxxvii]

Well, if the Democrats had been pussycats in their earlier questioning of Clarence Thomas, they now became pussy kittens, and for all worthwhile purposes they were muted in any real discussion of the charges brought by Hill. They abdicated their responsibility in an adversary system of government, and they abdicated their responsibility in the constitutional process of *advise and consent.* They fell back on their haunches and let the Republican members of the Committee have their way with Anita Hill, and the Republicans, with the consent of the President, were prepared to discredit her testimony in a most contemptuous manner. They were going to turn possible fact into total fiction.

The Republicans were also going to have their way for another reason. Some among the liberal Democrats would have trouble passing ethical scrutiny themselves. Senator Edward Kennedy was tainted from his

Chappaquiddick experience in which a young woman had died. Joseph Biden had admitted to plagiarizing speeches a few years before, and Dennis DeConcini had been investigated as one of the "Keating Five " in the Savings and Loan scandals that had swept the country in recent years. Indeed, DeConcini may have been influenced to vote with the Republicans for Thomas, in the seven to seven vote from the Committee, because he owed the Republicans for helping him get off lightly from a Senate Ethics Committee investigation.

Let me pause for a moment to clarify my analytic method at this juncture.

Much time has been spent here discussing the Judiciary Committee, its membership and politics. The information is important to know in this analysis, because it tells us how a reactionary, totally unqualified Supreme Court nominee was able to obtain Senate confirmation, even in the face of a charge of sexual harassment.

At the same time, it is important to know the lurid details of the sexual harassment charge, as told by Anita Hill, and it is even more important for the reader to know the intellectual, psychological and emotional response of Clarence Thomas to the charges. Looking at Thomas from both these perspectives will give us some clues to the psychological profile of the man that I described at the beginning of this paper.

However, before investigating Thomas' psychological profile, I will complete the discussion of the Republicans, response to Anita Hill's testimony.

After Anita Hill had delivered her prepared testimony on the first day of the second hearings, she then responded to questions from the Committee well into the afternoon. Thomas had the evening TV show of the hearings, and Hill was back the next morning to face questions from the Committee. The Republicans had used their first round of questions to probe Hill's testimony for weak spots. Based upon the probing they had done, they had now prepared a strategy to use against her, and they had their cannons loaded.

The Republican strategy against Hill was straightforward and unmasked. The word from the Prince was to attack Anita Hill and destroy her. Attack her testimony, her motives, her mind, her personality, her veracity, her integrity, her credibility, her blackness, and even her womanhood. Attack logically and attack illogically. Attack calmly and attack emotionally. Attack respectfully and attack disrespectfully, but with all means press the attack.

To help the Prince save face, the Republicans on the Committee had come to the hearing with the intention of punishing Hill severely, without physically hurting her. But short of that, all low-road tactics were stuck in the go position, which meant the use of gutter means: lies, distortions, and nasty character defaming innuendo. Accuse her of vindictiveness, jealousy, and of being an infamous "black bitch." Expose her as a conniving, emotionally stressed out woman who allowed herself to be used in a loathsome liberal plot to destroy the good name of Judge Clarence Thomas.

It is no exaggeration to say that because Anita Hill came across to the Committee, and probably to great numbers of the American people, as a credible, dignified, factual witness, the Republicans felt they had to destroy at best, or deeply tarnish at least, this image of a truthful woman. When it is her word against his, truth is in the eye of the beholder, and the Republicans wanted public opinion to perceive a negative when they saw or thought about Anita Hill. In the end, truth would be hard pressed to shine through, but one's perception would hit the eye like sunlight.

The task of denigrating and vilifying Hill was given to three of the Republican Senators. The assignment came directly from the White House, and passed on to Senator Thurmond, the ranking minority member of the Committee. Arlen Specter, Orrin Hatch, and Alan Simpson were told to blow Hill and her story right out of the water in whatever way they could. Specter was to be the interrogator, Hatch the inquisitor, and Simpson the abuser. Working together, they made a very despicable name for themselves in these Supreme Court nomination hearings.

Specter was up first, and he spoke calmly as he applied his prosecutorial experience and tried to use logic to weave patterns of deceit in Hill's testimony. To make his point he was not above browbeating her if she refused to accept his interpretation of events, and he found much fault with what he saw as her inconsistent behavior and illogical thinking, implying that a normal person would have done things differently. From his analysis, the Hill testimony should be discounted because the person who gave it was clearly irrational.

Most of Specter's questioning was much ado about nothing, and he searched like a lost person to find some point of significance to what he was doing, particularly when he could not legitimately shake Hill's story. Finally he badgered her about some speculative point that she gave an answer to but changed it later after thinking on it further. He accused her of "flat out perjury," and how happy he was to make that strong accusation against her. But, Senator Specter knew that he was just grandstanding for the TV cameras. As Joseph Biden had said, the Committee hearings were not likened to the proceedings in a court.

Only Ted Kennedy, later, challenged the notion that Hill had committed perjury, but by that time the damage was already done.

True to his religious upbringing, Hatch went after Hill like an indignant Mormon. Moral heresy and character assassination was occurring here by an untruthful, faithless woman. She was a Judas. She turned on a friend who only tried to help her at every turn. He knew that this woman had to be a liar because he had known Judge Thomas as a friend for ten years, and to get at his perception of the truth, Hatch saw nothing wrong with turning the Hill proceedings into an old-style inquisition.

Like heretics of old, Hill had to be exposed for the delusional, fantasizing, split-personality type of person that she was. She was probably not even aware of her own inner warped personality. Hatch described Anita Hill in just such terms, but he did not do it until she had left the witness table. If he believed so sincerely in Hill's dementia, why didn't he say it to her face? Who then was demonstrating a lack of moral fortitude?

Hatch also accused Hill of working in collusion with liberal groups of the worst kind, the kind that hire slick lawyers who know how to manipulate the truth and make bad appear good. Was this not always the case with the heretic? By name and nature, heretics were conspirators in league with evil and the devil.

Hatch took his best shots at Hill by strongly suggesting that she stole some of her most damaging testimony from the novel *The Exorcist* and an obscure, Midwest court decision. It did not matter that someone in the White House and an official at the EEOC had dug this information up for him, and he was just acting as a talking head. The information had to be correct because it fit the case. Anita Hill had been found out. How sad! Like most self-righteous people, to make his point, Orrin Hatch relied upon spurious data that masqueraded as fact.

As the public was soon to see, Specter and Hatch were the set up men for Alan Simpson. The first two would goad Hill into defensiveness, and then Simpson, the Wyoming cowboy, took her, one on one, in a street fight showdown. He was bigger and nastier than she was, and without the protection of the Democrats, he could bully and intimidate her as much as he liked. As a questioner, Simpson was illegitimate in the role. His real function was to throw dirt on Hill, to ridicule humiliate, abuse, and treat her with scorn.

Simpson was going to show the TV audience what a real man, a rugged individualist like himself, thought about such a vile person as Anita Hill. He was going to let everyone know that she was a sick, liar of a woman; and as a consequence, the American people would repudiate her. However, for him to be entirely effective in this role, he had to demonstrate his own anger and ill feeling towards Hill. The public had to see that he despised her.

Arching his back and practically putting his mouth into microphones in front of him, Simpson hurled innuendo and invective at Hill. Pete Hamill of the New York Post described Simpson this way: "At times, Alan Simpson looked clinically insane, the planes of his face moving in seven or eight directions at once, body arching, as he hushed with piety while reaching for papers that he said proved the perjuries of Prof. Hill. This slippery ambush artist..."[lxxxviii]

Simpson went on with his vituperation, castigating, maligning, and insulting of Hill, but his verbal assault did not cause her to lose her composure. She seemed to deflect his bitterness. This angered, and then enraged Senator Simpson. With her demeanor, she was making him look like a madman and a fool. Realizing that he was probably not succeeding at his intended purpose, he suddenly, in a last ditch effort to save himself, his deportment and his cause, went into a Senator Joseph McCarthy impersonation.

Gesticulating, with a cold, but excited look in his eye, Simpson, this self-described wild westerner, hinted darkly of Ms. Hill's "proclivities." William Safire of The New York Times said proclivities was a code word for homosexuality, and Mr. Safire went on to say that if Mr. Simpson had any evidence that Hill's sexual preference was related to her reluctance to bring a charge of sexual harassment, than he should have made the case or shut up. As a political conservative, even Mr. Safire was offended by Alan Simpson's behavior on the Judiciary Committee.[lxxxix]

The performances of the three Republicans who vilified Anita Hill were tawdry and vulgar. Their actions toward her proved to be an embarrassment to the Committee, the Republican Party, and the Senate as a whole. They were successful in smearing Hill, but they also denigrated their own reputations in the process.

But the blame here should not only rest on the head's of three immoral, self-serving, Senators. The Prince was involved with developing the strategy to savage Anita Hill, and Tom Wicker of The New York Times had this to say about that strategy. Even if President Bush and his White House Aides believed that Clarence Thomas was the victim of false charges, one must ask was it proper for the President and his men to launch in response a series of false charges of their own?

"Not only should 'the White House' and particularly the President hold themselves, and be held, to a higher standard of behavior than that, (but) they also could not know that Anita Hill was lying." What the President and his man did know was that the charges they concocted, that "she was fantasizing, she was a scorned woman, a disappointed careerist, perhaps mentally unstable, a participant in a conspiracy, were mere speculations (perhaps even fantasies) designed *on purpose* to discredit Anita Hill, to make her the issue rather then Clarence Thomas."[xc]

The President supported the use of gutter tactics against Hill, and they worked. The Republicans won the day, and in respect to the matter of sexual harassment, Thomas would be given the benefit of the doubt and presumed innocent of the accusation. But was this a proper assumption to make after all the witnesses were heard? And yes, there were other witnesses on both sides of the charge, even corroborating witnesses for Hill, four in all, a Judge, a law school professor, and two lawyers. But before the question of who was telling the truth is entertained, a final comment on those stoic Democrats on the Committee.

In the end, it was not the hard balling, smashing, bashing Republican assault an Hill that gave a public relations victory to Thomas and his supporters. The main reason for it was due to the reticent, complacent, frightened Democrats. They "were timid or cautious when they should have been bold and challenging. They allowed Thomas to set the terms of the discussion (ruling out all private questions) and never pressed him on his own flexible reputation for telling the truth."[xci]

The Republicans had asserted that Hill was suffering from delusions or schizophrenia, and the Democrats did not come to her defense. The Democrats were so hypocritical. They love to talk about gender and racial equality and sensitivity, but they seemed oblivious to the rape of Hill occurring right before their eyes. The poor liberals had been intimidated into silence by Thomas' manipulative charges of racism, and they seemed afraid to question Thomas aggressively for fear they would be perceived as unduly persecuting an innocent black man.[xcii]

But, was Judge Clarence Thomas innocent of the charge of sexual harassment? If this question were to be answered solely on the basis of a veracity quotient, Hill would be the winner. Thomas had a history of lying, fudging, and distorting the truth in testimony before congressional committees. He lied so much as Chairman of the EEOC, he did not know when he wasn't lying (see the commentary on Thomas and ADEA).

Thomas lied to the Judicial Committee in earlier testimony when he disavowed every political position he had ever taken. No one can relinquish his ideological convictions overnight. As the right wing newspaper columnist, Patrick Buchanan put it, Thomas tried to Uncle Tom his way past the Committee, and the strategy was a failure and a disgrace because it lost him votes in the Senate.

Thomas lied again when he said he had never discussed the Roe v. Wade case, in or out of Law School. Since everyone in the nation was talking about abortion rights, equating such rights with civil and constitutional rights, and Clarence Thomas had been Chair of the EEOC, the agency of government that had the primary function of enforcing civil rights in employment it is beyond incredible for him to say that the issue of Roe never came up.

More specifically, in a speech Thomas gave at The Heritage Foundation, a right wing Washington think tank, in June of 1987, he praised a recent essay by Lewis Lehrman, in which Lehrman spoke of a natural law, the law of God, which preceded "all institutions of human society and government."[xciii] Lehrman was trying to make the case that natural law supported the right to life idea of the antiabortionist groups and therefore natural law calls for an opposition position on the Roe decision. Lehrman specifically mentions Roe by name. Thomas' praise of Lehrman is because of his opposition to Roe. One could assume that Thomas agreed with that position, and he so told his audience that at The Heritage Foundation. Was this not discussing Roe?[xciv]

In the overall, Thomas lied about his relationship with Anita Hill. His response to her allegation of sexual harassment was that of stonewalling the Committee. "The precise truth of what went on in Clarence Thomas' office, and the exact nature of the relationship between Thomas and Hill, may never be known. But this much is clear: something happened.

"And that means Clarence Thomas, whose entire defense (was) that nothing happened, lied under oath to Congress, blatantly, repeatedly and with the entire nation watching."[xcv]

Something did happen between Thomas and Hill because he said so himself. "An initial FBI report indicated that Thomas had told the interviewer he had, in fact, asked Hill out but that she had declined and that was the end of it. When Thomas decided to change his story, the FBI interviewer did too, apologizing for his error in misquoting Thomas. C'mon, this interview was undoubtedly the most important assignment of the agent's career. It's hard to believe he was so careless on such an important question in a case of such prominence."[xcvi]

The Republicans tried to undercut the Hill allegation in many ways. For instance, they tried to make the case that sexual harassment is always exhibited by a pattern of abuse towards more than one woman, and Anita Hill was the only female accusing Thomas of such behavior. On its face, this was a very unsound proposition. If sexual harassment has anything to do with sexual fantasy, then its occurrence is more likely to be one to one. That is to say that one person can be uncontrollably attracted to another person or a particular type of person.

In any case, the Republicans were wrong. Another woman, Angela Wright of Charlotte, North Carolina did come forward to charge Thomas with sexual improprieties when they worked together at the EEOC. She was subpoenaed to testify before the Committee, but it never happened because the Republicans used up too much hearing time stroking Thomas and allowing his character witnesses inordinate opportunities to sell the good name of Clarence Thomas to the TV audience. Therefore, in the interest of time, the Committee accepted her sworn statement in lieu of verbal testimony.

If the Democrats had not been a part of this entire Committee hearing scam, and if they had not been sopping up to the Prince like the Republicans, Angela Wright would have come before that Committee to corroborate Anita Hill's accusations. But the Democrats did not want her to come before the TV cameras and tell a similar story akin to Hill's because her testimony, more then ever, would expose the fact that they, and Chairman Biden in particular, were guilty of nonfeasance throughout the entire proceedings that marked the nomination of Judge Clarence Thomas to the Supreme Court.

Angela Wright did not reach the witness table and neither did other witnesses who had testimony to give against Thomas in support of Hill. For example, Hill said that Thomas tried to have conversations with her concerning pornographic movies he had seen. Of course, Thomas denied it, but another woman, Lavita Coleman, recalled that in Law School Thomas enjoyed watching pornographic movies. Coleman had been a friend of Thomas during that time. He often discussed these films with friends.[xcvii]

If the Democrats had called Lavita Coleman to the witness table, very likely, Thomas would have been the loser. But no fear, the Democrats were now working in concert with the Republicans to keep explosive witnesses from testifying against Thomas. Mounting testimony against him would serve to underscore their pitiful incompetence.

Despite the inept performance of the Democrats, a great deal of potentially damaging information against Thomas appeared in the newspapers. There was no "smoking gun," but there was enough circumstantial evidence to say that he was not telling the whole truth about his former relationship with Anita Hill. It is very likely that something was going on between them as Hill said, and something did happen; or else, why was he stonewalling the Committee?

And what about Anita Hill, her veracity and so on? Well, there certainly was no public record of a pattern of lying. In fact, an opposite body of information hit the news media. Colleagues and people who had known her as far back as her days at Yale Law School vouched for and extolled the virtues of her integrity and truthfulness. She was just not the type of person to make up a story like this to derail Clarence Thomas' elevation to the Supreme Court, and the story itself supports this contention.

If Hill had totally fabricated her tale of sexual harassment, why didn't she make up a better story? This was a Law School Professor with a rational, legal mind. She knew the nature of adversary proceedings. She knew that she would be put on trial by the President's men. And given that the political stakes for the conservative Republicans were very high, she knew, having worked in Washington with Thomas, that they would come after her with a verbal sledgehammer. She knew that her integrity would be questioned, and they would discredit her at every turn.

Knowing all of this, why would she tell a story that could so easily be challenged for its inconsistency, its irrationality, its description of an emotionally stressed out woman who admits to using poor judgment in the matter, i.e., the fact that she went with Thomas to the EEOC after he had harassed her at OCR? If you don't believe that she was a pathological liar, the only other credible answer is that she told the truth; the flawed, frayed, illogical human truth. It was not a lawyer's truth, or an interrogator's truth, and certainly not a prosecutor's truth. It would be the truth of a powerless, professional woman who was working in a world dominated by men.

But, if Anita Hill was not convincing with her own testimony, she had four outstanding witnesses that corroborated her story. These four individuals did not know each other, and each decided to come forward on his and her own as a matter of conscience. They had never met before until they came before the Judiciary Committee. They were Susan J. Hoerchner, a judge in the Norwalk, California, office of the Workers' Compensation Appeals Board, a division of the California State Department of Industrial Relations; Joel Paul, a professor of law at American University in Washington; Ellen Wells, a lawyer and project manager of the American Public Welfare Associations and John Carr, a partner in the Wall Street Law firm of Simpson, Thatcher & Bartlett.

All four witnesses said that Hill had told them back in the early 1980s that her boss, who happened to be at that time Clarence Thomas, was sexually harassing her. The Committee heard this most corroborating and damaging testimony against Thomas, and its members as individuals, and as a body were totally unresponsive to this very strong support for Hill's allegations. This was a moral outrage. In the name of fairness, equity, and human decency, how could the Committee, Democrats and Republicans alike, not call for a halt to the confirmation proceedings until this matter was thoroughly investigated and cleared up one way or the other?

But, there was no call for a halt in the proceedings. Apparently, Anita Hill had performed an act of *time travel*. She had made up this story of sexual harassment in the present; then borrowed a time machine, gone back to the decade of the eighties; informed the necessary people about the story and came back to the present so these four people could testify in her behalf. Now that is fantasy messengers Hatch and Simpson, pure unreality.

But fantasy or not, Thomas would still get the benefit of the doubt because the Prince wanted it that way, and the second round of hearings came to a close. The confirmation vote would take place in two days, and neither truth, justice, or the American way would stop it from happening.

By a vote of 52-48, Clarence Thomas was confirmed as a Supreme Court Justice. It was the lowest margin of victory in the century, and because of all the controversy involved, a final postmortem is definitely in order.

On the eve of the Senate vote, national polls showed that 55% of men and 49% of women believed Thomas. Apart from the sexual harassment issue most Americans believed he should be given the Supreme Court seat. The reasons were varied and had much to say about the socio-political psyche of Americans.

In this regard, *Time Magazine* reported, "some Americans had to give up a few illusions about fair play and the complicated dynamics of racial and sexual solidarity. They learned that a woman who comes forward in good faith to make an accusation can become the accused, that skin color matters more to blacks then ideology, and that gender matters less to women than the causes women espouse in the name of feminism."

Nevertheless, if Hill's cause was just, why did most of the American people reject her testimony? *Time* went on to say that "some feminists argued that Hill lost the ideological battle in part because she lost the tactical one. For one thing, she missed prime time. 'Anita Hill spoke to 5 million Americans during the day. Thomas spoke to 30 million that night,' (said) University of Southern California law professor Susan Estrich. More important, perhaps, Hill's putative Democratic allies on the Senate Judiciary Committee sat back as judges while the Republicans played the role of prosecutors, ultimately painting the Yale-educated law professor as a delusional careerist," and "Hill was savaged for three days by Republicans who played to win. No one crossed-examined Thomas in the same tone."[xcviii]

Newsweek surveyed the situation and concluded that the willingness to believe Hill's testimony seemed to divide along class lines, but there was some difference of opinion about this. "While a Los Angles Times poll found no significant differences among working and nonworking women, education and professional standing proved a cutting edge: 31 percent of college-educated women opposed Thomas' confirmation, compared with 19 percent of nongrads. Nothing expressed that schism better than the testimony of J.C. Alvarez, Thomas' assistant at the Equal Employment Opportunity Commission. Alvarez portrayed Hill as an ambitious, arrogant careerist, while she herself came across as Every-woman."[xcix]

And what of black Americans who suffered very much from policies made and implemented by Thomas at OCR and the EEOC? Why did they give him such strong support? The nationally syndicated columnist Carl T. Rowan answered the question this way. Number one, there was a small group of blacks that believed in Thomas and really, no-holds-barred supported him. "They (were) his relatives and personal friends, and those black (neoconservatives) who believe that the certain route to political and financial success (was) to toady to George H. Bush and the Republican Party."

Number two, "a much larger group of blacks knew of Thomas' skin color, but very little about his criticisms and abandonment of the traditional, centuries-old struggle for black freedom. These blacks never gave up their view that if Bush was going to pack the court with another reactionary, it might as well be a black one. They accepted Thomas as the least threatening of possible new justices."

Number three, "Anita Hill's charges that Thomas harassed her sexually provoked powerful negative reactions among blacks, men and women, about a black woman bringing sexual charges that would deny a black man a position of power."[c] Because of ongoing racism, black men were suffering deeply. Their agony had become so severe in recent years; some social scientists have begun to say that black men have become an endangered species. Under these circumstances, Hill's behavior was totally unacceptable. The "evil black woman" takes on many different forms.

And in an odd, but realistic twist, Hill's case was also hurt by a segment of the black intellectual community that failed to rally to her support because they saw no significant difference between the establishment professor and the establishment judge. Neither was for the liberalization of America. "…Black Americans should have seen (that) something (was) wrong, something bizarre and unholy, inconsistent, as well as cynical and hypocritical for these (Senators), especially given their separate histories, to be promoting a Black man for a seat on the highest court in the land."

"It is safe to assume that within this context they have not changed philosophies: they have simply found one of their own in "living color."[ci]

"Given the nature of partisan politics in all this, it is again ironic that both of the leading players espouse conservative values, are champions of 'self-sufficiency', worked dutifully for the racist Ronald Reagan and supported the rejected Supreme Court nominee Robert Bork, who was thought to be a crypto-fascist.

"Clearly then, this (was) not a feud between two Black persons with diametrically opposed approaches to the struggle for Black progress and social justice in America. In short, this has not been the typical showdown between contending political philosophies. This was no liberal/moderate debate, as it should have been for it to have lasting historical value.

"Neither Judge Thomas nor professor Hill, caught in this vice of sexual politics, has demonstrated any desire to reform a judicial system rife with racism, inequity and corruption. Both are successful 'careerist' who will defend the system to the last iota because they both have vested interests in it…"[cii]

"The truth is that Clarence Thomas and Anita Hill (were) both cut from the same cloth. As byproducts of white America's elitist educational systems, they had come to believe that the American Dream was theirs, too. But even with their education, they knew they did not have equal access to that dream, so they agreed to be adopted, mentored and shepherded. And when one agrees to be shepherded, one plays the role of the sheep.[ciii]

"Black Americans bore witness to a bourgeois, negrified debacle that stressed the fact that Hill and Thomas were two sides of the same token. They were highly visible African-American conservatives who could be counted on to deflect criticism of the Reagan campaign to gut civil rights enforcement. And in this belated last act of their association, locked in corrosive opposition, they are once again being used against the interests of people of color, women and working people."[civ]

Given where they stood on the political spectrum, why should black America care about what happened to either one of them? However, at the same time, Blacks should care about Thomas because he is on the Supreme Court. Moreover, in his present position Thomas is a problem for all Americans because the character of his psychological profile will definitely be tested. Consider this: "The legal community has its own doubts about Thomas' ability to render neutral justice. This is the man who said 'an assassin's bullet' would have been preferable to the advice-

and-consent ordeal he was put through. How can Thomas be dispassion-
ate after he raged against liberal interest groups, Democratic Senators and
television cameras? What does he think of the First Amendment?...On
cases involving harassment, pornography and congressional power, will
Thomas seek revenge, or will he strive too hard to avoid the appearance of
conflict by ruling the other way?"[cv]

At the beginning of this paper I suggested that Clarence Thomas had
an abnormal psychological profile. This was indicated by his need to be
embroiled in controversy, his strong tendency for self-reference, his hard-
nosed attitude towards subordinates, and a perfectionist attitude coupled
with feelings of persecution. These patterns of behavior can be seen in the
conduct of his duties at OCR and EEOC and in his relationship with
Congress and the courts.

Some of his behavior as an administrator may have been planned as a
function of the Reagan revolution. How much did he do on his own and
when was he following orders? It is impossible to tell, but we can get some
further clues about his profile from the testimony he and Anita Hill gave to
the Judiciary Committee concerning her allegations of sexual harassment.

I said that Clarence Thomas, very likely, suffers from a disturbed, perhaps paranoid-like, psychological profile. There are two main elements to
this disturbance. One, the person submits to delusional type feelings of
grandeur; and two, he is disturbed by suspicious feelings of rejection or
persecution. According to Hill's testimony, and by his own behavior,
Thomas did display these tendencies.

For a man, sex and power go together. The sexier he believes himself to
be, the more powerful he thinks he is; and the more powerful he thinks he
is, the taller he can imagine himself to be above other men. This is fantasy,
of course, but for Thomas, who grew up under anomic conditions in the
fading days of white supremacy in the South, the longing to be powerful
must have begun at a very early age.

Pornography stimulates a man's sexual feelings, and thereby enhances
his sense of being powerful. Men are very attracted to pornographic films.

Vicariously, it can make them feel larger then life. Such sensations can easily feed a predilection for delusions of grandeur. Could this have been the case with Clarence Thomas?

Anita Hill testified to the fact that Thomas spoke to her about pornographic films, and Lavita Coleman said he enjoyed watching porno flicks because he discussed them with his fellow students. Hill said his conversations were very vivid and detailed, and he spoke of different films. Indeed, he spoke of them like a man who was a connoisseur of this type of film genre.

If what Hill told the Committee, and the comments from Coleman were true, then pornography was important to Thomas. This should have been a line of inquiry by members of the Committee because it could have been most revealing about the character and personality of the man in respect to his psychological profile. His testimony invited such an inquiry. He said, "I have been racking my brains and eating my insides out trying to think of what I could have said or done to Anita Hill to lead her to allege that I was interested in her in more than a professional way, and that I talked with her about pornographic or *X-rated films.*"[cvi]

According to Coleman, when Thomas discussed porno flicks he did it in vivid detail. One might gather from this that he was trying to impress his listeners with his knowledge of such "entertainment." Could this have been a way for him to raise his image in the eyes of others? Does it suggest a sense, and perhaps even an exaggerated sense, of self-importance.

Hill also told the Judicial Committee that Thomas on several occasions mentioned his own sexual prowess, and on other occasions he referred to the size of his own penis as being larger than normal.[cvii] Bragging about such matters with women is to deliver the message of sexual self-importance, and bragging is simply a more childish expression of delusions of grandeur.

On the other side of paranoid-like behavior, the person is disturbed by feelings of being persecuted. In responding to Hill's testimony, Thomas took the role of the injured party, and he then in the name of his *good name* spoke of himself as being under attack by Anita Hill, the Senate Judiciary Committee, and the nomination-confirmation process itself.

What nonsense! Hill had brought a serious charge against him, no doubt, and members of the press and the liberal, civil rights establishment had tried to dig up dirt on him, but that did not mean that everyone was against him as he characterized it. And most certainly the Committee and the process had been protecting him right along. But, when he used the expression of a high-tech lynching he completely destroyed whatever truth there was to his rebellious defense.

And he went on, practically shouting about uppity black men (something no one could accuse him of) and McCarthyism (something in his own way, he had been very good at as an agent for the Reagan administration) which unintentionally served to expose him for what he was, an *OpporTOMist*, who saw conspiracies approaching him from every quarter. And he had the nerve to say, "(Senators), you are ruining the country." Maybe Clarence Thomas doesn't kowtow to an old, liberal order, but he certainly does it for the new conservative one.

His outburst had all the earmarks of a person who felt not just accused, but persecuted. There is no telling how this man will function on the Supreme Court, but my feeling is that the other Justices will be less than collegial with him. They might even, in a subtle manner; treat him like the Pariah that he is. Two Justices have already admitted to having suspicions about their newest colleague.

Newsweek Magazine reported that two Supreme Court Justices believe that Clarence Thomas lied to the Senate Judiciary Committee when he denied the charge of sexual harassment brought against him by Anita Hill. The Justices were not identified, but the two told their clerks about their feelings.[cviii]

So, don't be surprised if in the near future, Thomas accuses his fellow Justices of a conspiracy to destroy his good name, and as well the good name of the Court, and even the good name of the nation. It is accusation that gives meaning to a paranoid's reality, and a paranoid loves to spread the blame around. As to his good name, such a conspiracy would be another example of a Thomasonian high-tech lynching of an uppity black man.

Conclusion

There, I have made my case. Associate Justice Clarence Thomas is morally and professionally unfit to sit on the Supreme Court of the United States, and since he will not resign, he should be impeached without delay. Moreover, he should be relieved of all his juristic duties immediately because his presence on the Court makes a mockery of any notion of the impartial administration of justice in our legal system. Furthermore, because he is a man of dubious distinction, without exaggeration, his place on the Court constitutes blight on the nation's conscience.

Beyond those negative points that I have already risen against Justice Thomas, there is a long list of other reasons why he should be removed from the High Court, forthwith. Indeed, it will be instructive to mention a few of them here.

Clarence Thomas has shown himself to be a very perturbed man when ever his behavior is questioned. Witness his outburst against the Judiciary Committee and the Supreme Court confirmation process, and it should be said that such behavior is indicative of a person who is likely to be hiding something.

Lacking qualifications, and against the odds, Thomas made it all the way to the Supreme Court. If he does suffer from delusions of grandeur, he has to be laughing at the American people, and he may be planning ways to get back at them for the hardships he has suffered early in his life and in the recent confirmation process. He certainly did not like the suspicions cast upon him because of the sexual harassment allegations from Anita Hill. He denied the charge, but there was still a public hearing. He defended himself, the people be damned. His integrity became a *four-letter word* that he hurled at the American people in defiance. Clarence Thomas is a very angry man and he will look for ways to vent that anger.

Thomas knows that he is no Thurgood Marshall, and he doesn't even think of himself as being black. He also knows that he gained his seat on the Court through lies, deceit and a monumental effort of submitting to the will of white sponsors, mentors and shepherds alike. In a racist society, that is practically the only way white men of power will accept a black man in their precincts of right wing politics.

With moral leadership so desperately needed in government, because Machiavellian political principles and methods are used to run the process, the American people will not be well-served by having an unconscionable individual in one of the most respected and powerful positions in our nation's polity.

Think of this, periodically when the public catches photographic glimpses of Thomas on the Court, they will be reminded of the *sleaze factor* in government, Watergate, the Iran-Contra Affair, and sexual harassment charges brought against a high government official. Undoubtedly, if Justice Thomas remains on the Court that body will lose some of its mystical power as one of America's most respected institutions. Rather than look up to the Supreme Court, Americans may begin to look down at it.

With all his talk about being a self-made man, Thomas owes his success to others, and consequently he is not a free-spirited, emotionally unencumbered type of person. This is to say that he has not been his own man since he allowed himself to be shepherded as a careerist in government.

Thomas may have been a demanding boss to his subordinates when he was an administrator, and he may have been negligent and arrogant to clients he was sworn to serve. Nevertheless, he was expected to obey the authority figures over him; those individuals with whom he plotted to undermine the civil rights mission of his governmental offices. As an *OpporTOMist*, behind that strong-looking black face, there lurked a very servile man. To go along, he had to get along, and that meant accepting his place in the pecking order of the Prince.

What the American people should be concerned about is how will this servile proclivity affect his decision-making as a Justice? Will Thomas, out of belief or habit, function to influence the Court to favor government interest over that of the individual? Thomas, because of his genuflecting past, may not be able to relieve himself of the attitude that he is a product of the ideological wars of government.

Some people may think that we should not be overly concerned with the attitudes of Justice Thomas because he is only one vote on a nine member Court, but the Court has already demonstrated in recent years that it is quite willing to circumscribe individual rights when they conflict with the power of government or other institutions of authority like the police.

Thomas' compromising nature will fit right in with kindred company. Moreover, one of the beneficiaries of this trend has been, and will continue to be, the office of the United States President. That office is our greatest, single symbol of government, and if we already have an imperial Presidency, what new Presidential heights will be achieved with the backing of a right wing Court that includes Clarence Thomas?

To be sure, speculation can stimulate our imagination, but the cold, hard reality of Thomas' unethical, immoral behavioral history can give us facts. It is a fact that this man mindlessly allowed himself to be used as a destructive force against the welfare of others. He was, in that Ibsen sense, *an enemy of the people*. He was used to help divide the country along racial and class lines so that the Reagan revolution could deliver more and more of the nation's resources to the rich elite while the needs of the poor, the working class, women, and the ethnic minorities were ignored.

Thomas is certainly a standard-bearer for the white-male elitist system that governs America. This is a conservative, old-boy network that is primarily concerned with one thing, vested interest. Its members hate the social philosophy of the liberals, and they do not encourage citizen participation in government affairs. Because it is easier to influence and control one person rather than many, they look to the President to be the dominant force in government.

The elitist old-boy network at the top of the social hierarchy uses standard-bearers like Thomas and others to help them hold on to the reins of power. They stay out of sight while manipulating ambitious paupers. These paupers attend top schools. They come to the professional world armed with theoretical and circular propositions and arguments that cannot be proved or disproved, but they are sure to generate debate. The upstarts will talk about God given "natural laws," survival of the fittest, social Darwinism, and noblesse oblige. And what is the purpose of all this talk? It is little more then rationalizations used by the few to control the many; and for status and money, the paupers will use these rationalizations to defend the vested interest of the elitist old-boy network that has empowered them.

As a member of the Supreme Court, Thomas, in his thinking, will depend upon the rationalizations that got him there; and as a consequence, his decisions will favor that conservative, old-boy network that holds power in America today. More than he even knows, he is extremely well suited to this role of a judicial lackey. The rationalizations that are indigenous to his professional, legal thinking will cause him to try to make decisions based solely on reason, and he will pretend to keep his personal feelings out of it. Therefore, feelings of fairness and equity for individuals and groups, not of the old-boy network, will be hesitatingly entertained, if at all.

However, here is the crux of the matter. As a Supreme Court Justice, Clarence Thomas constitutes a threat to the American people, in the long and short run. Because of his young age, he could be on the Court for forty years, and as a black reactionary he has been programed to maintain the status quo at all cost. Consequently, he has the mindset of a house negro who feels he must ingratiate himself with his master by turning on his own people and others of the same social background, class and predicament.

Truly, America cannot afford a Justice Clarence Thomas at this time. The nation is going through a series of class wars, as Pat Buchanan puts it, and new relationships must be forged. The haves must share more with the have-nots, but Clarence Thomas, inspired by his conservative mentors and the Reagan revolution has been fighting this reality. Metaphorically speaking, he is trying to hold back the dawn, and this makes him a socially disruptive force. He will not be a voice for liberalization, or moderation for that matter, on the present right wing leaning court. Indeed, he is likely to push for more reactionary decision-making.

For the American people to have a better chance in the future for racial and class harmony, societal peace and tranquility, Clarence Thomas must be removed from the Supreme Court. He is a troublemaker, and wherever he has gone bad times have followed. Consider this, in the final analysis, he is a symbol of elitism, suspicion and divisiveness, and these are the types of social forces that tear societies apart.

In the introduction of this paper, I asked the question, "Is democracy, as the founding fathers envisioned it, viable in America today?" My answer, based on the Clarence Thomas debacle, was no. I offered three main reasons for my answer: 1) The capitalistic, multicultural nature of the American polity, 2) racial politics, and 3) the strong influence of partisan politics in government affairs.

All three of the above reasons had a direct bearing on the outcome of the Thomas confirmation hearings, and in the aggregate they tell us a great deal more than most of us want to know about the internal workings of our government and the strong influence ideology plays in our politics. Let me explain.

To begin with, the Machiavellian nature of this nation's federal government process is well suited for the right wing politics that was used to get Thomas on to the Supreme Court. He was shepherded up the career ladder, and he received the nomination in large measure, because he was a conservative ideologue who bowed to the Danforths, the Prince, and the social philosophy of supply-side economics.

When his nomination seemed imperiled, Thomas' survival was helped by the fact that the racial politics of our polity prevented a political coalescence for Anita Hill. Once again, Americans had to learn an old, hard lesson, that race and class mean more to people in the United States than who is good or bad, right or wrong; and being white or black is more important to the individual than any sense of being an American.

In speeches and articles that he wrote, Thomas tried to deny the truths about our polity, but there is no doubt that racial strategies were very much involved in his career opportunities. To be sure, race was a major consideration for President Bush in nominating him to the Supreme Court, and when his nomination seemed swept away by a charge of sexual harassment, Thomas saved the day by playing the race card, which completely silenced the Democrats and brought more black and liberal support to his side.

However, ultimately Thomas was able to reach the Supreme Court because the President wanted him there. With extreme partisanship influencing governmental affairs, the President could pull political strings and manipulate Senators and public opinion. Party loyalties pitted Senators against one another, and their ideological differences became more an issue than the qualifications of Clarence Thomas. The Senate's responsibilities of the *advise and consent* role went right out the window once the President turned the confirmation hearings into a liberal vs. conservative prizefight.

All this activity was aided and abetted by the great American free press. What role did they play in this nomination battle? It can be said that they did not do very much. Yes, they were involved in the hearings, but really only as a recorder of the news. Except for the leak of Anita Hill's deposition to two news outlets, there was essentially no extensive investigative reporting done for this important Supreme Court nomination.

In an era of Hollywood exposes and mountains of celebrity trivia reporting, it is absolutely outrageous and an affront to the name of Thomas Jefferson that no serious, independent news investigation was conducted into the background and career of Clarence Thomas. If nothing else, you would have thought that the sexual harassment charges alleged by Anita Hill would have produced such an investigation, but it did not.

Never before was the voice of the news media so silent about an issue that could have such enormous impact upon America's future than it was with the Thomas affair. If just one of the major TV networks, or the New York Times, the Washington Post, or the Los Angles Times had done just a little research and discovery mission on the man's negative public record, the malfeasance in office, the refusal to carry out court orders, his failure to recuse himself on the Ralston Purina Case, and such findings were published, Thomas would never have been confirmed.

The news media should hang its head in shame for failing to do its duty in this situation, but the most astonishing fact about the failure of the news media is that all the information that would have disqualified Thomas as a nominee for the Supreme Court was a matter of public record. This was no Watergate occurrence, and there was no need for a "deep-throat" to help with the uncovering of a cover up. The news media was just plain guilty of a dereliction of duty. Moreover, this incident points up the fact that the government can easily manage the news in the face of a timid press.

The news media ignored a well-known dual axiom. Politicians are self-aggrandizing individuals by virtue of their aspirations and cynics by virtue of their profession. The fact that they are vote getters, and they must be crowd-pleasers, puts expedient behavior high on their performance list, and consequently their strongest motivation is self-interest; that is, getting re-elected. Therefore, what you see in politicians is never what you get. They are always ready to make a deal if it will help their re-election chances. This is to say that they are constantly participating in a world of hidden agendas.

The Thomas nomination-confirmation process was weighted down with its share of hidden agendas. The President used the nomination as a negative force to create an ideological fight on the Judiciary Committee and to split the black community. Southern Senators were destined to vote for Thomas no matter how unqualified he might have been because they were afraid to displease their black constituents. Arlen Specter tried to discredit Anita Hill because he wanted to raise his credibility with the most conservative Republicans in his party. He believed the right-wingers were going to try and defeat him in the next election because previously he had voted against the nomination of Judge Robert Bork.

Orrin Hatch, the moral Mormon went after Anita Hill with a "holier than thou" look flashing in his eyes because Senator Hatch also had a hidden agenda working. He was trying to cover up the fact that he had once been party to a memo that was written to criticize the government's sexual harassment regulations. The memo was sent to the same Clarence Thomas and one Andrew Lester, who were members of Reagan's transition team in 1980.

The memo was sent from the offices of Sen. Hatch, Sen. Richard Schwelker, R-Pa., and Rep. John Ashbrook. It said, "The vagueness of the definition of discrimination has undoubtedly led to a barrage of trivial complaints against employers around the nation." The memo went on to say, "The elimination of personal slights which contribute to 'an intimidating, hostile or offensive working environment' is a goal impossible to reach."cix

Having never held elected office, it cannot be said that Thomas was a politician, although throughout his career he worked closely with them. Nevertheless, he may have had his own hidden agenda connected to his rise to the Supreme Court. Even though he was not specifically a neoconservative himself, Thomas was one of the shining stars of the black neoconservative set which included individuals like Robert L. Woodson, Alan Keyes, and Michael L. Williams. His elevation to the Supreme Court was proof that a black conservative could succeed in the world of politics and government. Without a doubt, he was now the titular leader of the black neoconservative movement. He had become, in historian Stanley Elkin's famous words, a sambo for success.

All right, that is enough examples. Let us stop biting our tongues, and tell it like it is. If politicians are forever functioning in a world of hidden agendas, and our government is run by politicians, then our government is a tissue of lies, just as Clarence Thomas was a lie at OCR, a lie at the EEOC, a lie as an Appeal Court Judge, and now a lie as a Supreme Court Justice. Whenever and wherever the Prince holds power, the government that supports him will always be awash with lies.

Machiavelli was a cold-hearted realist. When discussing the functions of government, he suggested that Christian morals were inappropriate to the process. To follow that logic, it could be said that governments have been lying to their people for a very long time, if for no other reason then the fact that the people give them the authority to do so. However, lying governments are likely to be incompatible with the use of democratic institutions, and once the citizenry becomes susceptible to lies from their government, they are likely to lack the means for preserving their liberty. And, as every schoolboy knows, without liberty there can be no democracy.

In this regard, Eric Alterman says that the American people easily and readily accept the lies of government today. In contrast, he reminds us that when the American people realized that Lyndon Johnson had been lying to them about Vietnam, they forced him out of office. In a similar fashion, Richard Nixon was made to resign in disgrace because he lied about Watergate, but by the time we reach the Reagan Administration, lies had become just one more weapon in the arsenal of democracy. Reagan invented facts and figures and the press called them parables from "the great communicator." And what about George Bush's assertions? Was Clarence Thomas the best-qualified jurist he could find to sit on the Supreme Court? And, "was Saddam Hussein 'worse than Hitler?'"[cx] To both questions, we must respond with a resounding no!

Finally, allow me to paraphrase a well-known saying. It goes like this: There are lies. There are damn lies, and there are Princely lies. It was those Princely lies that gave us *Shamgate 91*, the biggest, most convoluted lie ever presented on national TV. It was one nasty, ugly, Joe McCarthy-type spectacle to behold. And where has it led us? Well consider this: Our so-called democracy can be judged on a sliding scale. As government lies go up, the possibilities for democracy in America go down. And to be sure, a lying government will make political paupers of us all.

AFTERWORD

Even though I believe that I have presented a solid case, an indictment, against Associate Justice Clarence Thomas of the Supreme Court of the United States, I harbor no illusions. I do not expect the Senate of the United States to impeach him. The reason is rather obvious. My indictment is as much against the political process in Washington, which includes the President and the Congress, as it is against Justice Thomas. To put Thomas on trial would be the same as putting the political process on trial, and this might expose the Machiavelli nature of the politics within the Beltway. It is no mystery, and there is little doubt, why the political system in our nation's Capital is so bad. It is self-serving, and the boys on the Potomac do not want the American people to think too hard about that.

However, in the words of Max Weber, the esteemed German sociologist, human behavior always produces unanticipated consequences. It was the Democratic controlled Senate that gave Clarence Thomas the votes to put him on the Supreme Court. How could the Democrats have known that one day Justice Clarence Thomas would be instrumental in giving the Presidency to the Republican candidate George W. Bush; and in doing so, cause the defeat of the Democratic candidate Al Gore. George W. Bush just happens to be the son of former President George H. Bush. How interesting. Apparently, when you make a pact with the Prince, it is forever, and it is never too late to honor a *quid pro quo*.

ENDNOTES

i. "A Report on the Nomination of Judge Clarence Thomas as Associate Justice of the United States Supreme Court," *National Association for the Advancement of Colored People* (NAACP), August 15, 1991, p. 19.

ii. Jerry Fresia, *Toward An American Revolution* (Boston, South End Press, 1988), p.61.

iii. *Newsweek*, "An Uncomfortable Seat," October 28, 1991, pp. 31-32.

iv. Ibid., p.32.

v. "Congressional Black Caucus Statement in Opposition to the Nomination of Judge Clarence Thomas to the Supreme Court," July 18, 1991.

vi. *Time*, "The Pain of Being Black," September 16, 1991, p.25.

vii. Ibid., p.26.

viii. Ibid., p.25.

ix. Ibid., pp. 25-27 (An *OpporTOMist* is Alvin Poussaint's mixture of the terms opportunist and Uncle Tom.)

x. Ibid., p.26.

xi. NAACP, footnote, p. 25.

xii. NAACP, p.6.

xiii. Transcript of Hearing in WEAL and Adams v. Bell, D.D.C., March 12, 1982, at 48, 52.

xiv. "A Critique of the Nomination of Clarence Thomas to the Supreme Court of the United States," *National Council of the Churches of Christ in the USA*, Summer, 1991.

xv. Letter from William Bradford Reynolds to Clarence Thomas, April 9, 1982.

xvi. *National Council of Churches*, p.5.

xvii. House Rep. 99-458, at 29, 27.

xviii.   34 CFR 106.51-61 (1975).

xix.   *National Council of Churches*, p.6.

xx.   North Haven Bd of Ed. v. Bell, 456 U.S. 509, 522 n.12 (1982).

xxi.   NAACP, pp. 29-30.

xxii.   Ibid., p.6.

xxiii. Ibid., pp. 49-51.

xxiv.   *See*, Remarks of Clarence Thomas, EEOC Law Seminar in Pittsburgh, Pa. (May 2, 1985).

xxv.   *National Council of Churches*, p.6.

xxvi.   Ibid., p.6.

xxvii. Clarence Thomas, "Affirmative Action Goals and Timetables: Too Tough? Not Tough Enough!" Yale & Policy Rev. 5:402, 403 (1987).

xxviii. Women Employed Institute, EEOC Enforcement Statistics, 1991.

xxix.   *National Council of Churches*, p.7.

xxx.   401 U.S. 424 (1971).

xxxi.   *The New York Times*, December 3, 1984, p.1.

xxxii. *Washington Post*, "EEOC to Resume Hiring-Goal Efforts," July 24, 1986.

xxxiii. *National Council of Churches,* p.9.

xxxiv. NAACP, p. 32.

xxxv.   Ibid., p. 34.

xxxvi. *The Los Angles Times*, October 11, 1988.

xxxvii. NAACP, p.36.

xxxviii. Speech to personnel/Equal Employment Management Conference, Department of Health and Human Services, November 16, 1983.

xxxix. NAACP, p.40.

xl.   Ibid., p.46.

xli.   *National Council of Churches*, p.10.

xlii.   Ibid., p. 11.

xliii. Ibid., p. 11.

xliv.   Hearings on the Nomination of Clarence Thomas to the United States Court of Appeals For The District of Columbia Circuit, Before The Senate Committee on The Judicary, 101st Cong., 2nd Sess. (1990), 189-90.

xlv.   *National Council of Churches*, pp. 11-12.

xlvi.   "I am Opposed to Affirmative Action!" Interview with Clarence Thomas, Chairman, EEOC by Chester A. Higgins, Sr. *The Crisis*, March, 1983, Vol.90. No.3 (The first part, "We Are Going To Enforce The Law," was published in February, 1983 edition of *The Crisis*.

xlvii.   *The Washington Post*, "Administration Asks Blacks To Fend For Themselves, December 5, 1983, p.A1.

xlviii.   Addressing the EEOC Committee of the ABA's Labor and Employment Law Section, Palm Beach Gardens, Florida, March 8, 1985.

xlix.   Thomas, "Affirmative Action Goals and Timetables," 403 n.3 (1987).

l.   Clarence Thomas, Letter to The Editor, *Wall Street Journal*, February 20, 1987.

li.   Thomas, "Affirmative Action Goals and Timetables."

lii.   Clarence Thomas, "Civil Rights as a Principle Versus Civil Rights as an Interest," in Boaz, D. ed., *Assessing the Reagan Years* (1988), 388-89.

liii.   Johnson v. Transportation Agency of Santa Clara County, 480 U.S. 616 (1987).

liv.   *The New York Times*, "Anger and Elation At Ruling on Affirmative Action," March 29, 1987, D1.

lv.   *The Washington Post*, "Despite Class-Action Doubts, EEOC Presses Bias Case," July 9, 1985.

lvi.   *National Council of Churches*, p.3.

lvii.   Ibid., p.3.

lviii.   Congressional Black Caucus, July 18, 1991.

lix.   NAACP, p. 3. & 5.

lx.   *Alliance For Justice Preliminary Report on Clarence Thomas*, July 1, 1991.

lxi.   Statement o the Leadership Conference on Civil Rights Opposing the Confirmation of Judge Clarence Thomas to the United States Supreme Court, August 7, 1991, p.2.

lxii.   Letter to President Bush from fourteen members of the House of Representatives, July 17, 1989.

lxiii.   *Alliance For Justice*, p.1.

lxiv.   Congressional Black Caucus, p.4.

lxv.   *National Council of Churches*, p.13.

lxvi.   Monroe Freedman, "Thomas' Ethics and The Court," *Legal Times*, August 26, 1991.

lxvii.   *The Supreme Court and Its Work*, Congressional Quarterly Inc. (Washington, D.C.), 1981, p.1.

lxviii.   Robert McClosky, *The American Supreme Court* (Chicago, University of Chicago Press, 1960), p. 27.

lxix.   Olive Taylor,, Two Hundred Years, An Issue: Ideology in the Nonimation and Confirmation Process of Justices to the Supreme Court of the United States, *Washington Bureau, NAACP*, September, 1987.

lxx.   Ibid., p.3.

lxxi.   Ibid., p. 3.

lxxii.   Ibid., p. 4.

lxxiii. *The New York Amsterdam News*, Black Skin, White Mask," October19, l991.

lxxiv.   *The City Sun*, Clarence Thomas or Anita Hill? Its Bad News Either way," October 16-22, p,12.

lxxv.   *The New York Times*, "A Wake-up Call to The Movement," October 14, 1991.

lxxvi.   *The New York Amsterdam News*, "Clarence Thomas: A Pyrrhic Bush Victory," October 19, 1991, p. 12.

lxxvii. *Standing Committee on Federal Judicary*, American Bar Association, March, 1991.

lxxviii. Letter (Report) to Chairman Joseph Bidens, Jr., Committee on the Judiciary, September14, 1991.

lxxix.   *The New York Times*, "Thomas' Judges: The Senate Panel," September 9, 1991.

lxxx.   *TheNew York Times*, "Judge Thomas Takes The Stand," editorial, September 9, 1991.

lxxxi.   *Time*, "Shame on Them All," October 21, 1991, p. 47.

lxxxii. *The New York Times*, "A Rehearsed Thomas is Set For Hearing," September 9, 1991, p. A12.

lxxxiii. *The New York Times*, "Who's Judge Thomas? For Now It Depends On Who You Are," September 8, 1991, Sect. 4, p. 4.

lxxxiv. John B. Harrison & Richard E. Sullivan, *A Short History of Western Civilization*, New York, Alfred Knopf, 1960, p.346.

lxxxv. David Broder, "Thomas TV Drama as Scripted," *Daily News*, October 21, 1991.

lxxxvi. *The New York Times*, "Prof. Anita F. Hill: I felt that I had to tell the truth," October 12, 1991, p. 11.

lxxxvii. *The New York Times*, "In An Ugly Atmosphere, The Accusations Fly," October 11, 1991, p. A1.

lxxxviii. *The New York Post*, "The Fun is Not Over Yet in This Seedy Drama," October 17, 1991.

lxxxix. *The New York Times*, "The Plot to Savage Thomas," October 17, 1991.

xc. *The New York Times*, "A Glorious Victory," October 16, 1991.

xci. *New York Post*, "Seedy Drama." October 17, 1991,

xcii. *The Guardian*, "Republicans: Anita's Mountain was a Molehill, October 23, 1991, pp. 5 & 18.

xciii. Clarence Thomas, "Why Black Americans Should Look to Conservative Policies," The Heritage Foundation, June 18, 1987, pp

xciv. Lewis E. Lehrman, "The Declaration of Independence and The Right To Life," *The American Spector*, April, 1987.

xcv. *Newsday*, "Stone Walling Won't Cut It," October 13, 1991.

xcvi. *The Guardian*, p.18.

xcvii. Ibid., p. 18.

xcviii. *Time*, "Woman Power," October 28, 1991, p. 24.

xcix. *Newsweek*, "Dividing Lines," October 28, 1991, p.24.

c. *New York Post*, "Key Questions About the Thomas Disaster," October 18, 1991.

ci. *The New York Amsterdam New*, "Clarence Thomas: A Pyrrhic Bush Victory," October 19, 1991, p. 12.

cii. *Amsterdam News*, "Black Skin, White Mask!" October 19, 1991.

ciii. *The City Sun*, "Clarence Thomas or Anita Hill?" October 16-22, 1991.

civ. *The Guardian*, "White Male Senators Expose Themselves," October 23, 1991. p. 4.

cv. *Newsweek*, "An Uncomfortable Seat," October 28, 1991, p.31.

cvi.   *The New York Times*, "Judge Clarence Thomas: My Name Has Been Harmed," October 12, 1991, p. 31.

cvii.   *The New York Times*, "Prof. Anita Hill," October 12, 1991, p.11.

cviii.   *Newsweek*, "An Uncomfortable Seat," p.31.

cix.   *Report From Congressional Advisors To EEOC Transition Team*, Jay Parker and Clarence Thomas, December 22, 1980.

cx.   *The New York Times*, "Democracy's Lies," November 4, 1991, p. A19.